computing
for
Adults

AN ESSENTIAL GUIDE FOR BEGINNERS

computing
for
Adults

AN ESSENTIAL GUIDE FOR BEGINNERS

Dr Alan Clarke

Hodder & Stoughton

A MEMBER OF THE HODDER HEADLINE GROUP

*To my wife and sons for their help and
support during the writing of the book
and particularly to Christine for her
correction of my grammar.*

Orders: please contact Bookpoint Ltd, 39 Milton Park, Abingdon, Oxon OX14 4TD.
Telephone: (44) 01235 400414, Fax: (44) 01235 400454. Lines are open from 9.00–6.00,
Monday to Saturday, with a 24 hour message answering service.
Email address: orders@bookpoint.co.uk

British Library Cataloguing in Publication Data
A catalogue record for this title is available from The British Library

ISBN 0 340 74327 1

First published 1999
Impression number   10 9 8 7 6 5 4 3
Year   2005 2004 2003 2002 2001 2000

Copyright © 1999 Dr Alan Clarke

Cover photos from Stuart Hunter, Debut Art and Amanda Hawkes
Typeset by Wearset, Boldon, Tyne and Wear.
Printed in Great Britain for Hodder & Stoughton Educational, a division of Hodder Headline Plc,
338 Euston Road, London NW1 3BH by J W Arrowsmith Ltd, Bristol.

Acknowledgements

The author and publishers would like to thank the following for permission to reproduce material in this book:
AltaVista; Bigfoot; Four11; 10 Downing Street; Microsoft Internet Explorer and Netscape Navigator.

Netscape Communications Corporation has not authorised, sponsored, endorsed or approved this publication. Netscape and the Netscape Communications Corporation logo are trademarks and tradenames of the Netscape Communications Corporation.

The AltaVista logo and Search Engine content are copyright and trademarks of Compaq Corporation. Used with permission.

All other names and trademarks are the reserve of their owners.

Contents

Introduction

There are many reasons for wanting to learn how to use a computer. You may wish to help your children with their school work, gain a new job, make sure you are not left behind or simply want to find out what surfing the Internet is all about. This book is intended to help you work towards these goals. It provides an introduction to a wide range of computer uses including word processing, spreadsheets, databases and the Internet.

This book is based on Windows applications such as Microsoft Word, Excel, Paint and Internet Explorer, with the intention of providing you with sufficient understanding to continue to develop your own knowledge and skills. These applications are widely used and amongst the most popular in the world. The opening chapter provides a foundation for those readers who have little or no knowledge and experience of computers. You should study this chapter before going on to those that concentrate on particular applications. However, you can choose to study the application chapters in the order that suits you best. Each one begins with a short statement of what you should be able to do after studying the chapter. This will help you to select which are the most appropriate for you.

Many adults gain their initial experience of computers through undertaking a basic Information Technology course. This book was written to support those taking part in their first computer course or who are simply teaching themselves. It should be useful in both situations.

The book was designed to be used in conjunction with a computer, so it is best if you read the book and undertake the exercises in front of the computer with the particular application (e.g. databases) running. You don't need to have any experience of the application before you start since each chapter begins by explaining how to load your chosen application. There are many practical exercises for you to attempt and you should do as many as you can since this is the way you will gain most benefit. In addition to the exercises, there are sets of self-test questions at the end of each chapter with answers at the end of the book. The language of computing contains many terms which will be new to you so a glossary is provided.

Computer systems can appear complex, but with perseverance you will be able to learn how to use the applications. Work through the chapters systematically and attempt each exercise. If it does not work first time then try again. Like most things in life, to become a competent computer user requires effort but is easier than many tasks you will have already successfully mastered.

There are many ways of configuring computers and a wide range of applications. This means that the computer you have at home or college may not be identical to the one described in the book. However, it should be broadly similar allowing you to transfer the knowledge in the book to your particular situation.

Dr Alan Clarke

Foundation

By the end of this chapter you should be able to:

■ Use a computer with confidence

■ List the component parts of a computer system

■ Use a mouse or similar input device

■ Use a keyboard

■ Describe the basic parts of the Windows 95 operating system

■ Understand the nature of software

■ Use your computer safely

This chapter is for those who have never used a computer before or who would like an overview of the hardware and software that make up a computer.

Most people who are using a computer for the first time are anxious: 'Am I too old to learn?' 'What do all these strange terms mean?' Almost certainly, you have accomplished more difficult tasks in your life than learning how to use a computer. If you are motivated to learn and willing to have a go then you will achieve your goals. The first step is simply to relax and if things are not clear at first keep trying – you will eventually understand.

The chapter is divided into three tutorials which include exercises that will allow you to practise many of the ideas presented in the text. They can be undertaken anywhere you can gain access to a computer – work, college, a local library or at home. Each exercise indicates how long it should take you to complete.

At the end of the chapter a series of short questions test your knowledge of computer hardware and software.

| Tutorial 1 | → | Hardware |

What is hardware?

The physical components which make up a computer are called the **hardware**. The main parts are:

- monitor
- memory
- central processing unit (CPU)
- magnetic disk (sometimes called the hard disk or drive)
- keyboard
- mouse
- disk drives (floppy and CD-ROM)
- printer.

Types of computer

Figure 1 shows a typical **desktop computer**. The two main components are the monitor (sometimes called a visual

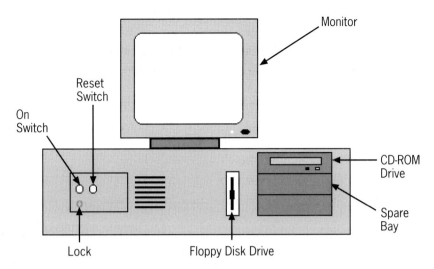

FIGURE 1 *A typical desktop computer*

display unit, or VDU), which looks similar to a television, and the large box which contains the computer's engine: the **CPU**, magnetic (**hard**) **disk** and drives. The CPU is the 'brain' of the computer.

Desktop computers are sometimes presented in a different style called a **tower**. Figure 2 shows a typical tower layout. The monitor simply sits on the desk alongside the tower. In both set-ups you should be able to see a number of features – floppy and CD-ROM drives into which you can insert the different types of disks, a power switch (this is sometimes

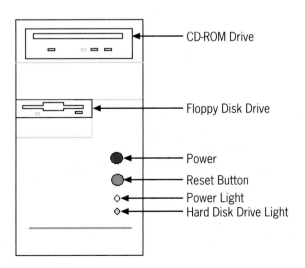

FIGURE 2 *A computer tower*

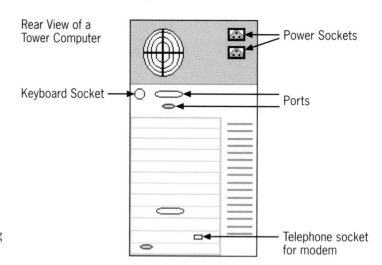

Rear View of a
Tower Computer

Power Sockets

Keyboard Socket

Ports

FIGURE 3 *The back of a computer tower, showing the ports*

Telephone socket
for modem

placed at the back of the box) and a reset switch. There are also some small lights to indicate that the power is switched on.

The back of the computer box provides the connections by which the different components are linked together by cables. The connections are called **ports**. Figure 3 shows the rear view of a tower.

There are other types of computer, which are called **laptops** and **palmtops**. A laptop is a portable computer with all the power of a desktop packed into a small case which opens on one edge to reveal a screen built into the lid instead of a monitor. A palmtop is even smaller than a laptop but usually does not have all the functions of either a laptop or a desktop computer. However, a palmtop computer can be carried in your pocket and is powered by ordinary AA batteries.

The monitor

The monitor (or VDU) provides you with a visual link to your computer. It is similar to a television and is available in a range of sizes: 14, 15 and 17-inch monitors are frequently used, although even larger ones are available. Figure 4 shows a typical monitor. The controls are similar to those on a television (contrast, brightness and controls for centring the display on the screen) and are often positioned at the bottom. On some monitors the controls are hidden behind a drop-down panel.

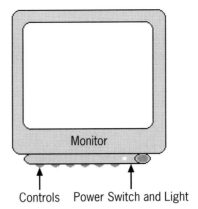

FIGURE 4 *A typical monitor*

What is a drive?

Drives enable you to read information stored on a **disk**. There are three types of drive:

- floppy
- CD-ROM
- hard.

Each uses a different type of disk.

A **floppy disk** is a flat rectangular plastic box containing a magnetic disk on which information is stored. When the disk is inserted into the drive, the information it contains can be read by the computer. Information can also be added to (usually called writing to the disk) and removed from the disk. A floppy disk can hold only a limited amount of information.

A **CD-ROM** is a computer version of an audio compact disc. It can hold a very large amount of information, the equivalent of several hundred floppy disks. Information is read by a laser beam within the drive and normally cannot be added to or removed from the disk. There are, however, special drives (called CD-R and CD-RW), which allow information to be added to and deleted from the disk.

Inside the computer is a fixed disk, which is called a **hard disk** or **hard drive**. It works in a similar way to a floppy disk in that it stores information magnetically. It will hold the equivalent of several CD-ROMs. It is possible to fit more than one hard drive to a computer, to increase the storage capacity of the computer.

The different types of drives in MS-DOS and Windows-based computers are identified by alphabetical letters. Floppy disk drives are usually designated as **A:** or **B:**, CD-ROM drives are often called **D:** and the hard disk inside the computer is usually known as **C:**. When you want to switch between drives you do so by changing letters within the Windows operating system (see Where are applications stored?). Other types of computer use different naming systems – for example, on an Apple Macintosh system you can give the drives whatever names you choose.

What is memory?

A computer needs a place to store and work on information. This is called **memory**. Computers have several types of memory:

- **Random access memory** (or **RAM**). This is the working memory in which the computer carries out its functions once it is switched on. RAM exists only while the machine is on – if the power is switched off so is the memory
- **Read-only memory** (or **ROM**). This is the computer's permanent memory and is built into the structure of the silicon chips inside the computer. It is not lost when the power is switched off
- **Storage**, where information and programs are stored as magnetic patterns on a disk.

When the computer is switched on, it uses its ROM to provide the basic instructions to set up the computer. It works on problems in RAM and stores the result on the hard disk or a floppy disk.

All forms of memory are measured in **bytes**. A byte is sufficient memory to store a single character (e.g. a letter or a number). Modern computers are often described in terms of their memory. For example, you may have seen the terms:

- 32 Megabytes of RAM (about 32 million bytes)
- a 4 Gigabyte hard disk (about 4,000 million bytes).

What is the CPU?

The CPU is the computer's equivalent of an engine in a car – it is the power within the computer. The CPU is a large silicon chip which fits into a circuit board called the **motherboard**. The key components of the computer (the hard disk, memory, keyboard, mouse and drives) all connect to or fit into the motherboard.

There are many different types of CPUs – for example, Intel Pentium MMX, Cyrix MX 200 and AMD K6 MMX. They are available in different forms depending on their speed (called the clock speed). A Pentium MMX 200 is more powerful than a Pentium MMX166 in the same way an 1800 cc engine is more powerful than an 1100 cc engine.

EXERCISE 1

Explore your computer

- Duration: 15 minutes

1   On your own computer identify the different components:

- monitor
- mouse
- keyboard
- floppy drive
- CD-ROM drive.

2   Look at the back of your computer and trace with your eyes how the cables link the different parts together. *Do not* touch them unless you have first isolated the machine from the power supply.

3   Try the monitor controls (e.g. brightness, contrast, vertical and horizontal hold).

How do you communicate with a computer?

The other common parts of a desktop computer are the **keyboard** (Figure 5) and the **mouse** (Figure 6). These are what you use to input data into the computer, which will respond by displaying information on the monitor screen.

■ THE KEYBOARD

With the keyboard you can enter text into the computer, in a similar way that you would use a typewriter to type words onto a piece of paper. The layout of the computer keyboard is

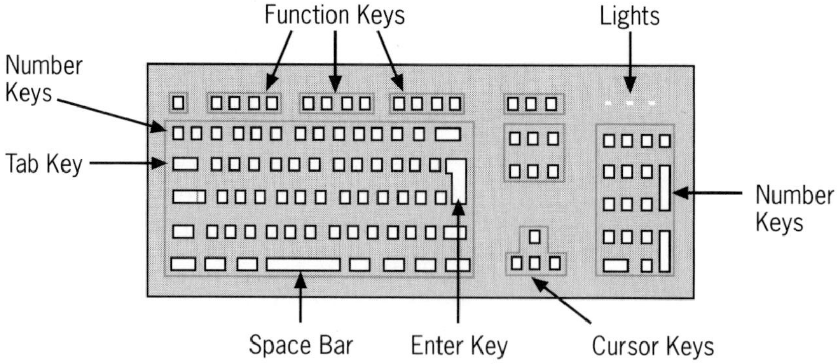

FIGURE 5 *A typical computer keyboard*

similar to that of a standard typewriter (e.g. the top line of alphabetical keys is QWERTYUIOP – this is why the keyboard is often called a 'QWERTY' keyboard). There are other keys which are also found on a typewriter – the space bar, capitals lock, a row of number keys towards the top of the keyboard, shift and punctuation keys. However, a keyboard has many more keys than you'll find on a typewriter. These include:

- a separate number keypad on the right (although laptops and some other keyboards don't have a separate number keypad)
- enter keys, which are used to confirm that you want to enter information into the computer
- a top row of function keys labelled F1 to F12 (but not all keyboards have these)
- a number of other special-purpose keys, whose role will gradually emerge as you work through the book.

EXERCISE 2

Explore the keyboard

- Duration: 15 minutes

1 Stand back from the keyboard and observe the overall layout. It is divided into four main areas:

- function keys across the top of the keyboard
- the number pad on the right of the keyboard
- the main QWERTY keys
- various other keys sandwiched between the QWERTY and number pad areas.

2 See if you can identify the special keys – such as Ctrl, Alt, Home, Pg Up and Num Lock. Eventually you will learn their

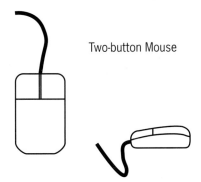

Two-button Mouse

FIGURE 6 *A two-button mouse*

purpose, but at the moment all you need is to start to gain an overall appreciation of the layout. This will help you once you start to use applications.

■ THE MOUSE

A mouse is a small, palm-sized device which is connected to your computer by a cable. The mouse is linked to an on-screen pointer (also called the **cursor**), which normally appears as an arrow and mirrors the movements made by the mouse. For example:

■ move mouse to the right and pointer moves to the right
■ move mouse to the left and pointer moves to the left
■ move mouse down and pointer moves down
■ move mouse up and pointer moves up.

On the top of the most common types of mouse are two buttons, although you may encounter mice with one, two, three or even four, buttons. By clicking on the buttons you can communicate with the computer, depending on where the pointer is positioned on the screen. This will be explained later – at the moment, just consider the physical device.

You operate a mouse button by resting your right hand over it, with your first finger on the left-hand button and your second finger on the right-hand button. The mouse is moved simply by pushing it around the mat (the mouse mat) it sits on. A mouse can be made suitable for left-handed users by making changes to the operating system.

Tutorial 2 → Using the mouse

The best way to understand a mouse is by using it. Exercise 3 provides you with the opportunity to practise. At first you may find it difficult but with practice most people become expert mouse users. There are five basic mouse skills you need to master.

1 **Moving** – accurate movement of the on-screen pointer.

2 **Clicking** (a single press and release of the left mouse button) – this communicates a command to the computer to start a process.

3 **Clicking** (a single press and release of the right mouse button) – this communicates a command to the computer to show some extra features.

4 **Double-clicking** (rapidly pressing and releasing the left mouse button twice) – this communicates a command to the computer to start a process.

5 **Clicking and dragging** – pressing the mouse button, but not releasing it, while the pointer is resting on an object on the screen and moving the mouse. The object will be dragged across the screen until you release the button.

EXERCISE 3

Using a mouse

■ Duration: 60

1 Switch on your computer.

2 Observe what appears on the screen. The computer checks itself as it goes through the process of switching on. You may see:

   ■ a memory test
   ■ a message – e.g. 'Starting Windows 95'
   ■ lights on the floppy and CD-ROM drives flashing to show they are being checked

The computer sometimes makes a noise like a small motor. This is the hard disk loading instructions and information into the computer, explaining how it should be set up.

3 After a few minutes you will see a display similar to the one

FIGURE 7 *The Start button and bottom-left hand corner of the Windows 95 display screen*

shown in Figure 7. It won't be *exactly* the same because the message depends on the computer and the software that is installed on the computer. However, in Windows 95 you will always see a Start box (this is called a **button**) in the bottom left-hand corner of the screen and a number of pictures with labels above it such as Word. These pictures are called **icons**.

4 Try to control the movement of the mouse around the screen but do not click either of the mouse buttons. If you do click by accident you may cause changes to the display. Move your mouse pointer to the four corners of the display. Position your mouse pointer over each picture on the screen in turn. Continue to practise until you can move the mouse pointer in straight lines and can position the mouse accurately over pictures.

5 With the mouse pointer over the **Start** button click the left-hand button and a new area, called a **window**, will open on the screen. Move your mouse until it rests on top of the **Program** option. This will be automatically **highlighted**. Now move the pointer to the right in a straight line and another window will open with a list of items. These are computer applications. Move the pointer up until it rests on **Accessories**, which will again be highlighted. Move the mouse pointer to the right and another list of applications will appear. Move right and down the list until you highlight **Games** and then move right again until you

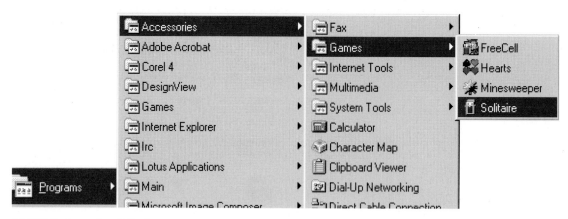

FIGURE 8 *Accessing Solitaire*

highlight **Solitaire** (Figure 8). This may take you several attempts. The key to success is to slide your pointer off the end of the item where the arrow is pointing.

You should notice a small arrow symbol pointing to the right at the end of each item. This is a standard feature of Windows 95 and indicates that if you slide your mouse off the end of the item another set of options will appear. Small arrows in Windows 95 always indicate that there are further options available if you slide your mouse pointer over them in the direction they are pointing (up, down, right and left).

Click the left-hand button while the pointer is highlighting **Solitaire** and a new window containing the game Solitaire will appear (Figure 9).

6 To play the game you need to master a complex set of mouse moves so it may take you several attempts.

7 The game will provide you with an interesting environment to practise using a mouse. The rules are the same as the card game solitaire. If you click with the mouse pointer on the pack of cards in the top left-hand corner, the cards will be turned over. You can move cards by positioning your pointer over the card and holding down the left-hand button. If you move the mouse now, the card will follow you until you release the button. For example, by holding down the button on the four of clubs in the pack you could drag it over the five of hearts and release the button. The black four will remain over the red five (Figure 9).

FIGURE 9 *Playing Solitaire needs some complex mouse moves*

8 Play the game. You are practising important mouse skills:

- moving the pointer
- single clicking
- clicking and dragging.

9 Continue until you feel confident in moving and using the mouse.

10 When you want to finish, move your pointer to the top right-hand corner, where you will see three small boxes (Figure 10). These are standard features of application windows in Windows 95. If you click on the X box you will shut down the game. The other two buttons **minimise** and **maximise** the application. Minimise reduces the application window to a small area on the bottom row of the screen. If you click on the resulting small window (button) the window will return to its original size. The maximise button expands the window to fill the whole screen. Practise minimising and maximising the window before you close Solitaire.

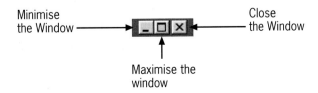

FIGURE 10 *Standard Windows features*

How do I switch off the computer?

Switching off the computer involves more than simply pushing the Power button (Figures 1 and 2). You must first shut down Windows 95. To exit Windows 95, click on **Start** and a window will appear in which the first item is **Shut Down**. Click on **Shut Down** and another window will appear in the middle of the screen with three options:

- **Shut Down**
- **Restart**
- **Restart in MSDOS mode**

You should see that alongside each of the options is a circle. In the one next to **Shut Down** there is a small dot. This indicates that this is the choice which will be enacted when you click on the OK button. If you want to change the option you must click in another circle. These circles are called **radio buttons** and are a standard feature of Windows 95.

Click on **OK** if the radio button is selected for **Shut Down** and you will see a variety of messages which indicate that the computer is closing Windows 95. Wait until a message appears telling you to switch off the computer.

Occasionally, usually because you have loaded some new software, you may need to use Restart, although normally the computer will tell you to do this (or, more often, it will do it for you).

You only need to use the third option (Restart in MSDOS mode) very rarely – in fact, you might never use this option.

Occasionally the computer will seem to freeze on you and nothing will work, with perhaps the exception of being able to move your pointer around the screen. This should be a rare event and if it happens frequently (more than once a day) you should seek help from your computer dealer. However, to get your computer to work again press the reset button on the desktop or tower. This is the manual equivalent of the Restart option.

Tutorial 3 → **Software**

What is computer software?

The **software** provides the instructions to make the hardware work. It allows specific tasks to be performed such as communicating with the Internet, keeping records or writing letters. Computers need to match hardware and software together so that they work in harmony. To ensure that the match is exact, a special software program (called an **operating system**) is needed. This provides a foundation on which **applications software** can work. The operating system provides all the standard features such as saving information onto the hard and floppy disks, printing documents, linking the keyboard and mouse to the application and presenting the information on the monitor.

A wide range of operating systems are available. The most popular systems for personal computers (PCs) are MS-DOS, the Macintosh system and Windows. This book is based on Windows 95. Windows 95 is loaded automatically when the computer is switched on.

What are windows?

Applications such as word processors are run within a defined rectangular area of the screen called a **window**. Windows can be moved, expanded in size or made smaller on the screen so that it is possible to run several applications at the same time. Figure 11 provides an example of a Windows display with three applications shown in separate windows.

A windows environment contains a range of standard features which allow you to use the operating system. These standard features are:

- icons
- menus
- buttons
- radio buttons
- arrows
- folders and directories.

These will be explained to you in later parts of the book.

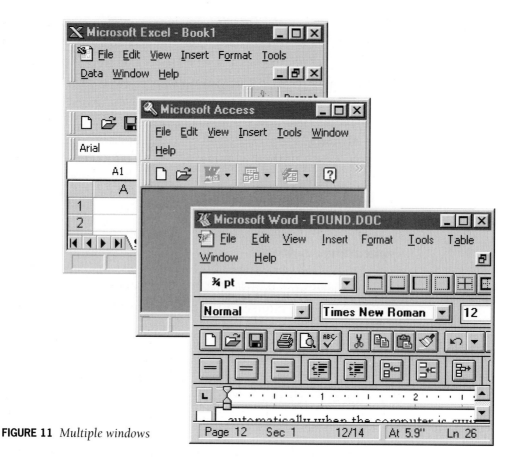

FIGURE 11 *Multiple windows*

How do I start an application?

You can start an application in two main ways.

On the opening Windows 95 display (Figure 7) there is a button called Start in the bottom left-hand corner and a range of small pictures (icons) across the rest of the screen. Figure 12 shows the icon for Microsoft Word, a popular word processing program. If you position your mouse pointer over the icon and double-click the left-hand mouse button you will activate the word processor.

Double-clicking requires you to click the left mouse button twice rapidly. It can take a little practice to get the speed right. If nothing happens when you first try to double-click keep on trying – eventually it will work.

Buttons and icons are similar in that if you click or double-click on them you will start something happening.

FIGURE 12 *The Word icon* Windows 95 is largely based on the concept of pointing at

objects with the mouse and clicking on them. Sometimes just placing the pointer over an object will cause things to happen (e.g. placing it over the Start button will cause the message **Click here to begin** to appear). You need to explore and experiment with the mouse.

As explained in Exercise 3, you can also click on the Start button and choose Programs, then slide your mouse right and either up or down until it is over the item you want and click on it. The application will be activated and open up on the screen. There is normally more than one way – and in some cases three or four methods – of doing everything in Windows 95. *You* decide which approach suits *you* best. There is no right answer.

Figure 13 shows you what Microsoft Word 97 looks like when it is activated. It can appear as a small window, similar to those in Figure 11, or it can fill the whole screen. You can change a small window into a large one by clicking on the maximise button (shown in Figure 10). If you click on the button again the window will return to its original size.

Figure 13 also illustrates **scroll bars**. A window can be bigger than the display, both vertically and horizontally and in order to view the contents of the window you use scroll bars on the right and bottom edge of the window. You can see that they begin and end with a button marked by an arrow. If you click on the arrow, the display will move in the direction of

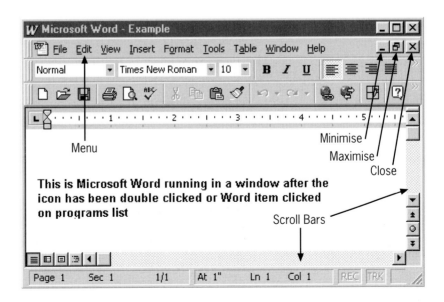

FIGURE 13 *A Microsoft Word window*

the arrow to reveal the contents of the window. This is called **scrolling**. It is like unwinding a roll of paper, but you can scroll to the left and right as well as up and down. If there are no scroll bars visible then it simply means that there is no hidden content.

How do I close an application?

There is more than one way of stopping an application.

You can simply click on the close symbol in the top right corner of the window. The window will close and the application shut down at the same time.

Another way is to use the menu that appears on the top of the application window (**File Edit View Insert Format Tools Tables Window Help**). If you click on **File**, a list of choices will drop down and the last item is **Exit**. The application will close down if you click on **Exit**. You may have noticed that some letters of the menu and other items (e.g. **Programs**) in Windows are underlined. Using the keyboard, if you press the letter that is underlined and the Alt key together, it will have the same effect as clicking on the items with the mouse. This is called a **keyboard shortcut**.

EXERCISE 4

Exploring Windows

■ Duration: 45 minutes

1 Windows is a complex and interesting operating system that provides you with a useful working environment. It is important to become familiar with Windows since it has many standard features which all Windows applications make use of, such as loading applications, saving files, printing and manipulating windows.

2 Clicking on **Start** opens up a menu of options which includes **Programs**. If you position your mouse or click on Programs then a list of options opens up to the right. Move your mouse right and click on **Accessories** which opens up another list of options to the right.

This includes **Tips and Tour**, which you should click on. A window (shown in Figure 14) is displayed, which contains a guided tour of Windows. It is possible to install Windows so that this tour appears every time you switch on your computer or so that it is installed as part of the Help function (click on **Start** and

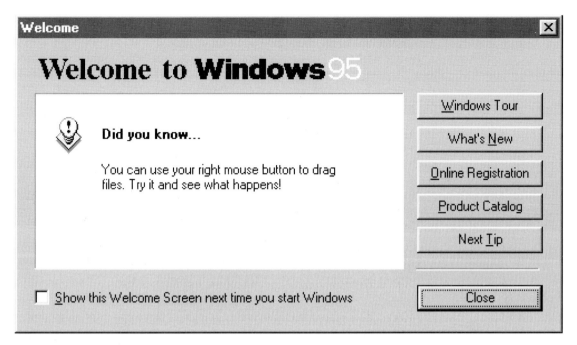

FIGURE 14 *Tips and Tour*

Help to access the tour). Access the tour whichever way is easiest for you.

Clicking on **Windows Tour** will take you into a tutorial aimed at introducing you to Windows. Follow the instructions on the screen and work through the introduction. The tour provides you with an introduction to many of the issues which later chapters will develop.

3 Take your time and take notes of the issues that interest you.

How is applications software supplied?

When you buy a new application you are given either a number of floppy disks or a single CD-ROM. Load the disks into the appropriate drive.

A floppy disk is inserted with the metal cover first and uppermost into the drive. You push it until it all disappears inside the drive. If it does not go in with a minimum amount of resistance then it is likely you have it the wrong way round. A floppy disk is removed from the drive by pressing the button on the front of the drive.

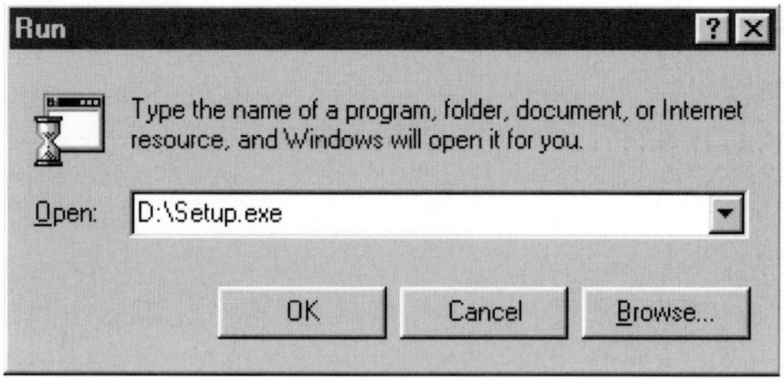

FIGURE 15 *Loading software*

A CD-ROM is loaded by opening the drive by pressing a button on the front of the drive and placing the disk into the drawer with the decorated side uppermost. Push the drive button again and the CD-ROM will be taken into the computer.

How do I load software?

Software is supplied on either floppy disks or CD-ROMs, which must be inserted into their respective drives. The software can usually be loaded onto the computer using a special routine called Set-up, which is stored on the disk containing the software application. If you click on **Start** and then **Run**, a dialog box (Figure 15) appears. In this case, a CD-ROM has been inserted into the drive, which is called **D:**. If you enter **D:\Setup.exe** and then click on **OK** the application will start to load. You need to follow the instructions which appear on the screen. These will often ask you questions which at first may not mean a lot to you; however, the loading sequence will always suggest an answer and if you are in doubt simply agree with the suggested answers.

If your application is on a floppy disk then you would enter **A:\Setup.exe** (**A:** is the floppy disk drive).

There are other approaches to loading applications offered by Windows 95. In some cases, the operating system will recognise the presence of a CD-ROM and will automatically reveal the run box with the set-up instruction waiting for you to click on **OK**.

When you buy a new computer the software applications are often already loaded for you.

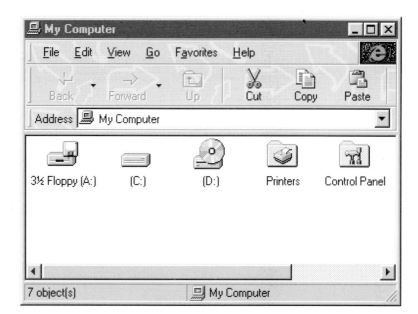

FIGURE 16 *The My Computer screen*

Where are applications stored?

Software (e.g. applications and files) is stored on the internal hard disk, which is usually known as the **C:** drive. You can locate **C:** by double-clicking on the **My Computer** icon, which appears when the computer is first switched on (it is often located in the top left-hand corner of the screen). The window that opens after you double-click will be similar to the one in Figure 16 and will contain a series of icons, some of which represent the disk drives:

A: floppy drive
C: hard disk (which, confusingly, is also called a drive)
D: CD-ROM drive.

Software is stored on the computer in a series of **folders** and within each folder are the individual components called **files**. This keeps the software organised so you can find it. Each folder and file is given an individual name.

In Windows, all files end with a full stop and a short **extension**. The extension tells you what type of software the file holds. For example:

- .doc, .txt and .rtf are examples of files that hold text
- .exe is a file that holds a program which carries out an action when it is loaded.

What is the structure of the folders?

Even a new computer is likely to have a number of folders that contain the operating system, accessories, games and applications. They can appear confusing. However, *all* computers store folders in a structured, hierarchical way, deciding on a general folder in which to place other more specific folders of files that are related to the general subject. In turn, the specific folder can contain other folders. This is very similar to creating a filing system of papers. The aim is to enable you to find your files again. This is very important because after you have been using a computer for even just a few months, you will discover that you have produced many new files.

What is a menu?

A **menu** is a means of providing you with a list of choices from which you can select. Menus appear when you click on a button and are often organised in groups called **bars** along the top of a window (see Figure 13). A typical Windows menu bar will contain

File   Edit   View

If you click on **File**, **Edit** or **View** a list will open up below the button. For example, if you click on **File** you'll see the following choices:

File   Edit   View
New
Open
Close
Save
Save as

A shortcut alternative is to press the Alt and F, Alt and E or Alt and V keys. Remember, wherever you see the letter underlined, you know that a shortcut consisting of the Alt key and the underlined letter is available.

EXERCISE 5

Explore folders structure

■ Duration: 30 minutes

 Folder Icon

System

 File Icon

Subscriptions

 File Icon

Acrocat

 File Icon

_syminst

 File Icon

025790

FIGURE 17 *Folder and file icons*

1 Double-clicking on **My Computer**, which appears when your computer is first switched on, will reveal the display shown in Figure 16.

2 Double click on **C:** and a window will appear showing you the folders stored on your hard disk.

3 Double click on the Windows folder (you might have to scroll up and down the window to locate the folder) and a large number of other folders will appear, showing you the number stored within the Windows folder. If you explore the window by scrolling both vertically and horizontally you will see that there are files as well as folders. Folders are shown by a yellow record card icon, whereas files have a variety of icons. Figure 17 shows some different icons. Remember, there are several ways of displaying folders and files so don't worry if your display is different from this.

4 Double-click on the system folder and another set of folders will appear. These are folders within the system folder, which in turn is inside the Windows folder. If you look at the top of the display you will see a line called **Address** with **C:\Windows\System** in a box alongside it. This is called the **path**. It tells you that the system folder is inside the Windows folder and that both are stored on internal hard disk (**C:**) drive.

5 If you click on the **UP** icon on the toolbar you will move up one level to the Windows folder (the Address will change to **C:\Windows**).

6 Look at the menu bar at the top of the display and click on **File**, then place your mouse pointer on top of **New**. A list of options will appear to the right, including the option **Folder**. If you click on **Folder** you can create a new folder. This will be inserted into the folder you have open (i.e. if you are in Windows with Address showing **C:\Windows** your new folder is placed in the Windows folder).

7 Click on **Folder** if you have not already done so and a new folder will be created. You might have to scroll around the window to locate it. It will be highlighted and will initially be

called **New Folder**. Enter Examples as the name of the folder. You have now created a new folder called Examples inside the Windows folder. Click on **Examples** and you will see an empty window open.

8 Click on the **Close Window** button on each window that is displayed until you return to the desktop with the **My Computer** icon.

How do I save information?

The approach to saving your work is the same in all Windows applications, so you can apply the same technique over and over again. It is based on the concept of saving any piece of work as a file. A computer file is a like its paper equivalent – it is a place to store information. Saving is important because if you switch off your computer without saving the work you have completed it will be lost. In most cases you will save it to the hard disk, though you can also use a floppy disk.

In all Windows applications, if you click on **File** and then **Save** a dialog window will appear (see Figure 18). This shows you the folder in which your file will be saved and the other files that are already in that folder. You can change folders if you want. Before you save your file you need to give it a name.

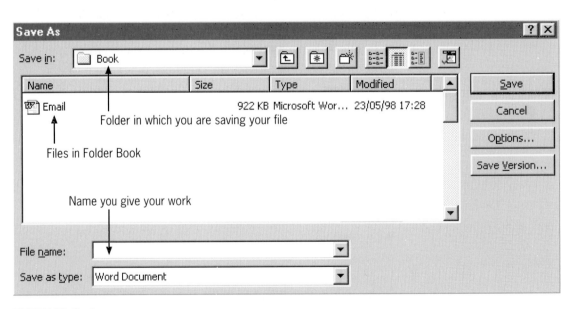

FIGURE 18 *Saving*

It is always best to give it a meaningful name so that you can find it again easily. You will be given several opportunities to practise saving later.

How to use your computer safely

There has been a great deal of publicity about the very real dangers of using a computer. However, there are some straightforward steps you can take to reduce risk and increase your comfort.

Give yourself space

You need enough space to be comfortable. You need room for your legs and desk space for books, guides and disks with the freedom to change the position of the keyboard, mouse and monitor. A good test of layout is that you can use all your books, keyboard, mouse *and* see the screen without excessive twisting of your body. Change the layout until you are comfortable.

Use a suitable chair

Chairs should be adjustable and you should alter the height and backrest until you are comfortable. Your lower back needs to be supported and you should be able to place your feet on the floor or on a foot rest with your knees slightly higher than the chair to ensure good circulation of blood. The height of the chair should allow your eyes to be slightly below the top of the screen and you should view the screen from a distance of at least 18 inches.

Reduce strain

You can reduce the strain on your hands and wrists by:

- Keeping your wrists straight while typing (e.g. by using a wrist rest)
- Not resting on your wrists
- Typing gently without excessive force
- Taking frequent breaks and avoiding typing for long periods.

Adjustable back support

Space in front of keyboard to rest wrists and forearms

Height and angle of monitor can be adjusted for most comfort

No strains on thighs or knees

Enough space under desk to move around

Adjustable seat height

Wheels on chair for changing position

Foot rest

FIGURE 19 *Organising your workspace safely and comfortably*

Use correct lighting

Try to position your screen so it does not reflect light from the sun or artificial lights. You should adjust the brightness and contrast of the monitor to meet your needs. If your computer is illuminated by natural light, position it at right angles to the window. If the room is illuminated by artificial light then tilt the monitor so that reflection is minimised.

What next?

This chapter has introduced you to the basic hardware and software that makes up a computer system. To become a competent user requires lots of practice. This book contains many exercises which you should undertake – they will provide you with the experience you need to become an effective computer user.

SELF TEST QUESTIONS

If you want to test your understanding of this chapter try to answer these questions. The answers are given at the end of the book.

1 What are the most common types of computer you are likely to encounter?

2 What does A: represent?

3 What does one byte of memory hold?

4 If someone used the word 'QWERTY', what would they be talking about?

5 Two of the standard Windows features are minimise and close. What is the third feature?

6 How do you load the operating system?

7 How do you start an application?

8 In Windows, how can you tell that a keyboard shortcut is available?

9 How are applications programs supplied?

10 What should all Windows files end in?

Word processing

2

By the end of this chapter you should be able to:

- Describe the functions of a word processor

- Create and amend a document

- Change the characteristics of a document (e.g. font and character size)

- Alter the layout of a page (e.g. change margins)

- Use a range of functions, including:

  - copy and paste
  - cut and paste
  - insert and overwrite
  - bold, italics and underline
  - find and replace
  - spell checking
  - insert clip art

A word processor allows you to produce professional-looking documents such as letters, reports and homework without being an expert typist. It provides help with spelling, allows you to change your mind without having to start again from the beginning and lets you print one or more copies of your finished product.

Word processing is probably the most popular of all computer applications because it is useful to almost everyone. If your handwriting is difficult to read then you can produce high-quality documents every time. If you find spelling a problem then the built-in spell checker can provide you with an immediate improvement. If you have to write a lot of similar documents it allows you to reuse your work. Figure 20 shows part of a letter being written on a word processor.

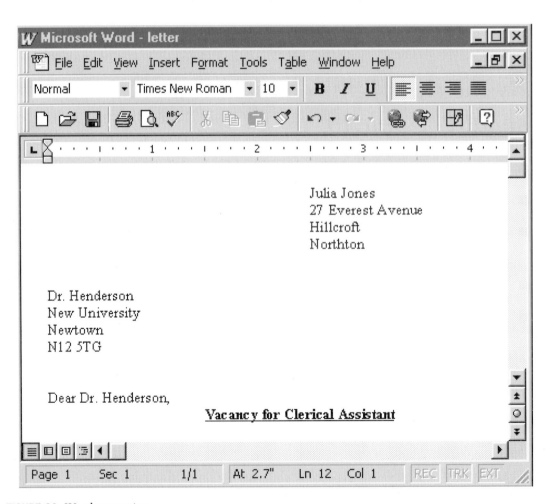

FIGURE 20 *Word processing*

Word processing has changed the lives and jobs of many office workers. In 1980 many organisations employed specialist typists, who spent their days typing documents which had been drafted by other people. In 1998 there are fewer typists but many people word process their own correspondence. On train journeys it is now a common sight to see travellers using their laptop computers.

There are many different word processing applications. Here are a few:

- Word for Windows (Microsoft)
- Corel WordPerfect (Corel)
- Lotus Word Pro (Lotus).

There are now also several word processors which allow spoken input – so you don't even have to be able to type!

Tutorial 4 → What is a word processor?

Figure 21 shows you the main features of Microsoft Word that appear when you first load the program.

Most word processors are similar in appearance and

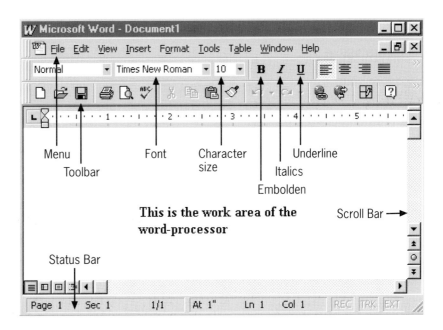

FIGURE 21 *The main features of Microsoft Word*

provide the following basic functions. The screen consists of three main areas:

1 A menu and a **toolbar** at the top. These provide you with the controls to design your documents. They may appear complex at first, when they are new to you. However, you will soon find that they are not difficult to understand or use.

2 The **work area**. This is the area into which you enter the text and pictures that will form your document.

3 The **status bar**, which is at the bottom. Read it from left to right:

Page 1 The page you are on. Documents can be as long as you like.

Sec 1 The section of the document you are currently working on.

1/1 Shows you that you are looking at the first page of your document, which is one page long.

At 1″ Tells you that you are entering text that will appear 1 inch below the top of the page when it is printed.

Ln 1 You are entering text into the first line of your document.

Col 1 You are entering text in the first character position of the document.

EXERCISE 6

Explore your word processor

■ Duration: 60 minutes

1 Double-click on the **Word** icon and the software will load. A small hourglass will appear alongside the mouse pointer to show you that the software is loading.

2 A screen appears for a moment or two telling you that you have loaded Microsoft Word 97, but this is rapidly displaced by the word processor screen. This may occupy the whole or only part of the display screen. If it occupies only part of the screen (i.e. it is in a window) then click the maximise button in the top right-hand corner of the window (see Figure 10 if you can't remember where this is). The word processor will now fill the screen.

3 In the work area you will notice a flashing vertical bar. This is

called a **cursor** and tells you where the text will appear. If you move the mouse over the work area it changes shape from an arrow to an **I** bar. If you move the mouse over the menu, toolbar or status areas it turns back into an arrow.

4   Enter your name and address. For example:

Janet Smith, 17 Townsend Lane, Norris Green, Liverpool LS1 4GH

You will observe that the cursor moves with your text and that the **Col** item in the status bar changes with each character entered.

5   If your name and address is longer than one line, the text will automatically **wrap** around. This means that the text will move to a new line without you having to do anything. On a typewriter you have to start a new line with a carriage return but a word processor does this automatically. If you *do* need to insert a new line then press the enter key. Continuing to press enter will insert more blank lines.

6   Look at the toolbar and observe what it tells you about the font and size of character you are using (see Figure 21). There are lots of different fonts available for you to use – if you click on the down arrow button to the right of the font box a list of them will appear (an arrow indicates that more options are available). The list is in the form of a **scrolling window**. If you scroll down or up you will see many different names of fonts (Ariel, Balloon, Times New Roman and so on). Pick one by clicking on the font name. The name in the font box will change to the one you have just chosen. Type in your name and address again and see how it looks in the new font. Here are some examples:

■   Futura Book:
     Janet Smith, 17 Townsend Lane, Norris Green, Liverpool LS1 4GH
■   Tekton:
     Janet Smith, 17 Townsend Lane, Norris Green, Liverpool LS1 4GH

7   The character size can also be changed by clicking on the down arrow next to the size box and selecting the size you want. Try it. For example:

character size 12 – Janet Smith

character size 24 – Janet Smith

8 Explore the options that are available under the menu items (e.g. **File**, **Edit** and **View**). See if you can locate:

- new
- open
- save
- print
- undo
- copy
- paste
- zoom
- font
- paragraph
- spelling.

These are some of the useful functions which modern word processors provide. You should expect to find these features in all word processors but not necessarily under the same menu items.

Under the **View** menu is an option called **Toolbars**. This allows you to change the functions available on the toolbar. Be careful how you use this – it can alter the appearance of your application so that options disappear! New users often find this confusing. You should see that you are using the Standard and Formatting Toolbars only. You will be using these toolbars throughout this chapter.

9 If you rest your pointer over the toolbar without clicking, a small message will appear to explain what the button does. See if you can find these:

- new
- open
- print
- spelling
- cut
- undo
- center
- top border.

You may have noticed that some of the toolbar items are duplicated under a menu. In almost all programs you have more than one way to perform an action. There is no right way – *you* choose the way that *you* prefer. You may see that some of the toolbar icons are faded (this is called **greying out**). This means that they are not available at the moment.

Tutorial 5 → Getting started

How do I get started?

When you first start Microsoft Word, the work area is blank except for the flashing cursor, which is positioned on the start of the first line of the new document. You can also see another short horizontal line below it. This line shows the end of your document – and, since you have just started a new piece of work, it is on the next line. The word processor automatically gives your work a name – if you look on the line above the menu you will see it has been called **Document 1**. This is a temporary name which you can change later. You usually change the name of your document when you save the file.

EXERCISE 7

Entering and deleting text

■ Duration: 45 minutes

1 Enter the text below, or choose another short passage to enter.

Battle of Rorke's Drift

The battle of Rorke's Drift is best known by many people through the film *Zulu*. It was an amazing event, in which a small garrison of men armed with modern weapons defeated a large force of men armed with assegais and shields. The victory was more remarkable in that a whole British army had been defeated by the same Zulus earlier that day. For part of a day and a night the Zulus attacked but could not penetrate the fortifications which were constructed of sacks of grain. Eleven soldiers were awarded the Victoria Cross, Britain's highest military medal, for their actions at Rorke's Drift.

2 Note how the text starts a new line when it needs to without your doing anything. This is called **word wrapping**. If you have

been trained as a typist you might find it difficult to stop yourself trying to create a new line. Do not worry if in your work area you are not able to get the same number of words per line as in the example. This is due to the settings within the word processor, and you can change these later. Simply enter the text.

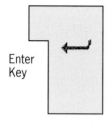

Enter Key

3   If you want to start a new line you need to press the enter key. This is the key with the bent arrow.

4   The cursor should be flashing at the end of the word 'Drift'. If you press enter, watch the cursor move to the start of the next line. If you press enter again your cursor will move down another line, showing you now have a blank line. Enter your name in this line and you should see, for example:

actions at Rorke's Drift.
Janice Jones

5   Try clicking on the down arrow of the scroll bar and watch the text moving up the screen. Clicking on the up arrow will bring the text back.

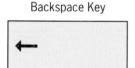

Backspace Key

6   It is often necessary to remove or delete text. There are two main ways to do this. Look at the screen – the cursor should be flashing at the end of your name. If you press the backspace key then the cursor will move to the left and delete the last character. If you continue to tap the key, you can delete your entry.

Del

7   The other way of deleting text is to use the delete key which is located in the bottom right-hand corner of the keyboard near the number pad.

The delete key works by removing the characters to the *right* of the cursor.

In your text the cursor probably does not have any text to its right. However, reposition the cursor by moving the mouse pointer (shaped as an I bar) until it is at the beginning of your name and clicking once. By pressing the delete key now, the text to the right will be deleted. Continue to do this until you have removed your name. If you find that instead of deleting the letter you have inserted a full-stop you need to press the Num Lock key once before continuing.

8   Save your document as a file. This process is the same in all Windows applications, so you can save a spreadsheet, database and graphic image in exactly the same way. If you click on **File** and **Save** then a window opens – it is shown in Figure 18. In the box **File name:** enter **c:\Windows\Examples\Exercise7** (click in the box to allow you to enter text) and then click on the **Save** button on the right side of window. Your document will be saved as a file called Exercise7 and will be stored in the Examples folder you created in Chapter 1, which is in turn stored in the Windows folder.

9   If you want to save your work on a floppy disk then insert one into the drive and enter **A:\Exercise7** into the **File name:** box and click **Save**.

How to lay out your page

When you are writing with a typewriter you must work in a logical sequence. You must decide on the layout of your document before you begin. You need to decide what margins to leave and once you have begun you can change your mind only at the cost of beginning again. However, with a word processor you can make decisions at any time and change your mind as often as you want.

To lay out a document you need to click on **File** and then **Page Setup**. A window which resembles a set of record cards (Figure 22) will appear. Alternatively you can use the keyboard shortcuts indicated by the underlined letter (e.g. F for File and u for Page Setup which you need to press together with the Alt key).

If you read the top card – **Margins** – you will see the words **Top**, **Bottom**, **Left** and **Right** on the left-hand side. These represent the **margins** on all four edges of the page. A margin is the gap between the edge of the paper and the start of the text. A preview of how the text will appear is presented in the centre of the card. If you want to change the margins you must click on the up arrow next to that particular margin to increase or the down arrow to decrease the size (alternatively, you can delete the text in the box and type in what you want). You will see the preview change as you increase or decrease your margins, and the figures in the boxes will change.

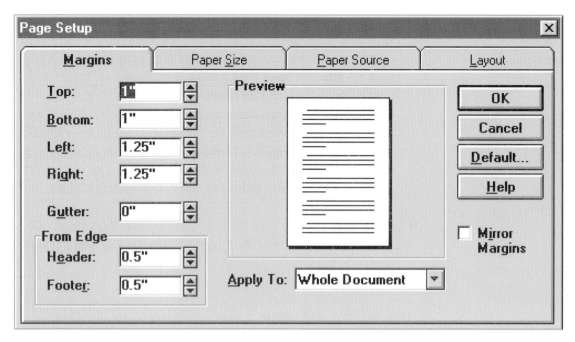

FIGURE 22 *Page setup record cards*

EXERCISE 8

Page layout

■ Duration: 30 minutes

1 Click on **File** and then on **Page Setup**

2 Explore what happens when you change the four margins.

3 Observe what happens on the preview.

4 The other record cards (e.g. **Paper Size**) can be accessed by clicking on the record card tabs. For the moment it is not important what these cards contain.

On the **Page Setup** cards you will see three other layout devices:

■ **gutter** – this is the extra space that has to be allowed for facing pages to be bound together (see Figure 23).
■ **header** – this is essentially a standard item which is placed at the top of each page. It is often a graphic, such as a company logo, but it can be text only or a mixture of text and graphics (see Figure 24).
■ **footer** – a footer is used in the same way as a header but is placed at the bottom of each page.

Gutter Margins

FIGURE 23 *Gutter margins*

A useful feature of a word processor is that it allows you to **justify** your text. There are four options:

■ left justification – the passage is aligned so that all the words start at the left margin, but the lines are ragged in the right-hand margin
■ right justification – the passage is aligned so that all the words finish at the right hand margin, but are ragged at the left-hand margin
■ centre justification – the passage is aligned so that the middle words are aligned with the middle of the page, and the lines are ragged at both ends
■ full (or double) justification – this is a combination of both right and left justification, and the text lines up smoothly at both ends of the line.

Examples of justification are shown in Figure 25. You choose the justification you want by clicking on one of four icons shown in Figure 26.

You can change the justification of a passage by using a technique called **highlighting** and then clicking on the icon representing the new alignment.

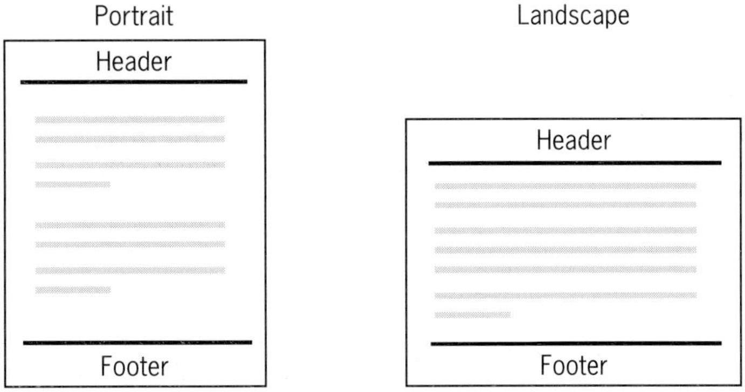

Portrait
Header

Landscape
Header

Footer

Footer

FIGURE 24 *Headers and footers*

Left justification:
This is a passage which is aligned to the left. It is left justified. This is a passage which is aligned to the left. It is left justified. This is a passage which is aligned to the left. It is left justified. This is a passage which is aligned to the left. It is left justified. This is a passage which is aligned to the left. It is left justified. This is a passage which is aligned to the left. It is left justified. This is a passage which is aligned to the left. It is left justified. This is a passage which is aligned to the left. It is left justified. This is a passage which is aligned to the left. It is left justified. This is a passage which is aligned to the left. It is left justified.

Right justification:
This is a passage which is aligned to the right. It is right justified. This is a passage which is aligned to the right. It is right justified. This is a passage which is aligned to the right. It is right justified. This is a passage which is aligned to the right. It is right justified. This is a passage which is aligned to the right. It is right justified. This is a passage which is aligned to the right. It is right justified. This is a passage which is aligned to the right. It is right justified. This is a passage which is aligned to the right. It is right justified. This is a passage which is aligned to the right. It is right justified. This is a passage which is aligned to the right. It is right justified.

Centring:
This passage is aligned so that the middle words are aligned with the middle of the page. It is centred. This passage is aligned so that the middle words are aligned with the middle of the page. It is centred. This passage is aligned so that the middle words are aligned with the middle of the page. It is centred. This passage is aligned so that the middle words are aligned with the middle of the page. It is centred. This passage is aligned so that the middle words are aligned with the middle of the page. It is centred. This passage is aligned so that the middle words are aligned with the middle of the page. It is centred.

Full justification:
This passage is fully justified. It is a combination of right and left justification.
This passage is fully justified. It is a combination of right and left justification.
This passage is fully justified. It is a combination of right and left justification.
This passage is fully justified. It is a combination of right and left justification.
This passage is fully justified. It is a combination of right and left justification.
This passage is fully justified. It is a combination of right and left justification.
This passage is fully justified. It is a combination of right and left justification.

FIGURE 25 *Justification*

What is highlighting?

Highlighting is a method of marking a part of your document so that you can change it. It involves using the mouse. Place your pointer at the start of the area you want to change and hold down the left-hand mouse button. Move the cursor to the end of the area and you will see the background colour change from white to black. When you reach the end of the material you want to highlight, release the mouse button. You can highlight a single word or many pages.

With the text highlighted you can change many of its features – such as font, character size and justification – simply by choosing the new characteristic and clicking the mouse once with the pointer away from your highlighted area. If you make a mistake, click on Edit and then Undo. This will

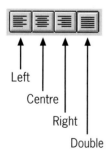

Left
Centre
Right
Double

FIGURE 26 *The justification buttons*

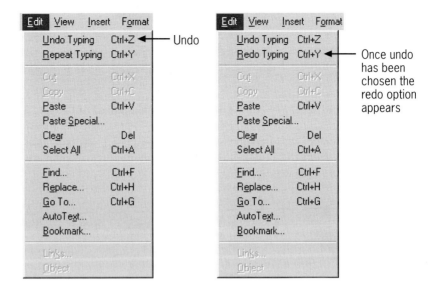

FIGURE 27 *Undo and redo*

undo your last action. You can use Undo repeatedly to undo a series of steps. Equally useful is the Redo option, which appears as soon as you have used Undo once. The two choices allow you to easily correct mistakes (Figure 27).

Many applications have an undo facility. It is normally found under the Edit menu.

Tutorial 6 → Other features of word processors

Word processors provide a number of other facilities to change and manipulate your documents. These are very useful in that you can experiment with your documents after you have written them. You are not committed to getting everything right first time. This allows you to improve your presentation. The main features are:

- copy and paste
- cut and paste
- insert and overwrite
- bold, italics and underline
- find and replace
- spell check
- insert clip art.

Cut, copy and paste

Copy and paste are the means of copying words from one part of a document to another. This can be extended using the cut and paste function, which allows you to remove some words from one place and put them in another. They are the computer equivalent of taking a pair of scissors and physically cutting out a section and gluing it in another part of the document.

EXERCISE 9

Copy and paste/ Cut and paste

■ Duration: 1 hour

---

1 Enter the text below (or choose another short passage to enter).

Interaction

Interaction is the element of screen design which is often ignored. This is probably due to its having no obvious physical presence. However, its role is crucial since the value of an interface is judged by the users in terms of interaction (i.e. is it user friendly?).

Information presented by a book or television is essentially a one-way communication. The viewer or reader is affected by the communication but has no direct way of influencing the communication except to switch off or stop reading. In contrast to these media, the computer has potential to allow two-way communication.

Computers have the capability to meet the needs of their users since they can receive feedback from them and react to it. The principal means of creating this feedback or two-way communication is through the use of the control system.

The degree and style of the interaction which each control approach provides varies considerably. The main options are command entry, menus, form fill, natural language and direct manipulation.

2 Use copy and paste to move text around the document. First of all you must highlight the text that you want to manipulate.

Position your mouse pointer at the start of the first paragraph (beginning with 'Interaction is the') and hold down the left-hand mouse button. Move your pointer to the end of the paragraph ('i.e. is it user-friendly?') and release the button. Your text should be highlighted – the letters will be white and the background black. Now click on **Edit** and then **Copy** (see Figure 28). The highlighted text should not change yet. Move the mouse pointer

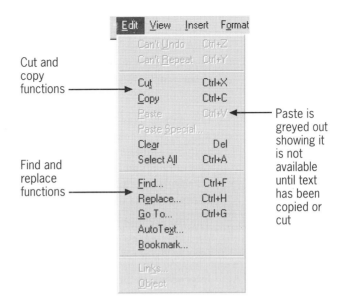

Cut and copy functions ⟶

Paste is greyed out showing it is not available until text has been copied or cut

Find and replace functions ⟶

FIGURE 28 *Using copy and paste and cut and paste*

to the end of the text ('language and direct manipulation') and click once. The highlighting will disappear. Click on **Edit** and then **Paste** (see Figure 28). The text you have copied will now appear and you now have two identical paragraphs. If you have any difficulties try again.

This copy and paste operation will work with a single character, a word, a sentence or a whole document. It is very useful when you want to change your work. You can paste your copied text anywhere in the document.

3   The cut and paste operation is very similar. Highlight the sentence 'However, its role is crucial, since the value of an interface is judged by the users in terms of interaction (i.e. is it user-friendly?)'. Click on **Edit** and then **Cut** (see Figure 28). Your highlighted text will disappear. Move the mouse pointer to the end of the third paragraph ('The principal means of creating this feedback or two-way communication is through the use of the control system.') and click on **Edit** and then **Paste** (Figure 28). Your text will reappear.

4   Your document should now read:

Interaction

Interaction is the element of screen design which is often ignored. This is probably due to its having no obvious physical presence.

Information presented by a book or television is essentially, one-way communication. The viewer or reader is affected by the communication but has no direct way of influencing the communication except to switch off or stop reading. In contrast to these media, the computer has potential to allow two-way communication.

Computers have the capability to meet the needs of their users since they can receive feedback from them and react to it. The principal means of creating this feedback or two-way communication is through the use of the control system. However, its role is crucial, since the value of an interface is judged by the users in terms of interaction (i.e. is it user-friendly?).

The degree and style of the interaction which each control approach provides varies considerably. The main options are command entry, menus, form fill, natural language and direct manipulation.

Interaction is the element of screen design which is often ignored. This is probably due to it's having not obvious physical presence. However, its role is crucial, since the value of an interface is judged by the users in terms of interaction (i.e. is it user-friendly?).

5   Continue to practise highlighting, copying, cutting and pasting. Move some single words, sentences and other-sized chunks. Do not worry if you make a mess of this passage.

6   Save your document as a file. Click on **File** and **Save** – a window like the one in Figure 18 will open. In the box **File name:** enter **C:\Windows\Examples\Exercise9** and click on the **Save** button. Your document will be saved as a file called Exercise9 and stored in the Examples folder you created in Chapter 1. This in turn is stored in the Windows folder.

7   If you want to save your work onto a floppy disk then insert one into the drive, enter **A:\Exercise9** into **File name:** and click **Save**.

Insert and overwrite

Insert and overwrite are two **modes** of operation. In insert mode, you can place extra words into the document without affecting the existing text. In overwrite mode, your new words appear on top of the existing ones so that they disappear.

For example:

Starting point: *Insert and overwrite are two modes of operation.*

Using insert: *Insert and overwrite are two **I am inserting** modes of operation.*

Using overwrite: *Insert and overwrite are two **I am inserting** ation.*

FIGURE 29 *The INS key*

1 You can use only one of these functions at a time and you move between them by pressing the INS key which you will find on the bottom row of the numbers key pad to the right of the keyboard.

2 Enter the text below:

Second Thoughts

Second Thoughts was originally a Radio programme which was so successful that it was turned into a television series. It told the story of two adults who were developing a relationship in spite of the problems of her teenage children and his ex-wife. Both of them had previously been married so this is their second chance.

3 Make some changes using insert. Position your mouse pointer after 'Radio' and type in a space and '4'. Move your pointer to after 'series' and enter a space then 'with Lynda Bellingham and James Bolam'. Insert, which is the normal mode of operation, allows you to place new words in the passage. The surrounding text is moved automatically to make room for the new words.

4 The overwrite mode is enacted simply by pressing the INS key. Press the key once (if you press it twice it will revert to insert mode) and position your pointer in front of '4' and type Four. Observe what happens. You *should* see 'originally a Radio Fourogramme'. The text does not make room for the new word and you can easily make a mess of your words. Press the INS key again to return to insert mode. In most cases you will use insert but overwrite is occasionally useful if, say, you want to remove a few words.

5 The status line (see Figure 21) changes when you are in overwrite mode. If you look at the right-hand side of the line at the bottom of the display **OVR** will be highlighted if you are in overwrite mode. However, you might notice you have pressed the key accidentally only when you begin to overwrite your words. You can recover from the mess by using the undo option. You will need to use Undo for each character you have changed: keep clicking on Undo until everything returns to normal.

6 Practise with insert and overwrite until you feel confident.

7 Save your document as a file. Click on **File** and **Save**: a window (shown in Figure 18) will open. In the box **File name:** enter **C:\Windows\Examples\Exercise10** and click on the **Save** button on the right-hand side of the window. Your document will be saved as a file called Exercise10 and stored in the Examples folder you created in Chapter 1, which is in turn stored in the Windows folder.

8 If you want to save your work onto a floppy disk then insert one into the drive and enter **A:\Exercise10** into **File name:** box and click **Save**.

Bold, italics and underline

Bold, italics and underline are three **presentation** options. You can choose them in any combination:

This is bold text
This text has been emboldened and set in italics
This text is emboldened, in italics and underlined.

EXERCISE 11

Bold, italics and underline

■ Duration: 30 minutes

1 Please enter the text below:

Isaac Asimov

Isaac Asimov was one of the leading science fiction writers of the twentieth century. He produced outstanding factual and science fiction books and stories from the 1930s to the 1990s. Throughout his life he wrote almost continuously, producing over 400 books.

2 You can find the three functions bold, italics and underline on the toolbar just to the right of the character size box. If you highlight the title of this short passage ('Isaac Asimov'), click on **B** for bold and then click elsewhere you will see that the title is

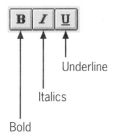

FIGURE 30 *The bold, italics and underline buttons on the toolbar*

emboldened (**Isaac Asimov**). Highlight the title again, click **U** for underline then click elsewhere – the title is now underlined as well (**Isaac Asimov**). Highlight it a third time, click on **I** (for italics) and then elsewhere. The title is now shown in bold, italics and underlined (***Isaac Asimov***).

3 You will notice that the B, I and U buttons change appearance once clicked. This shows that the functions are on. To switch them off you click on them again. Experiment with switching them on and off. You can use one, two or all three functions in any combination. If you enter text from the keyboard when a function is on, the text entered will be in that function or combination of functions. Try entering

Is this bold, italics or underlined?

with any or all of the functions on.

■ if bold is on, you'll see **Is this bold, italics or underlined?**
■ if italics is on, you'll see *Is this bold, italics or underlined?*
■ if the underline function is on, you'll see <u>Is this bold, italics or underlined?</u>
■ and if bold, italics and underlined are all on the text will look like this: ***<u>Is this bold, italics or underlined?</u>***

4 Save your document as a file. Click on **File** and **Save**. A window like the one in Figure 18 will open. In the box **File name:** enter **C:\Windows\Examples\Exercise11** and click on the **Save** button (right side of window). Your document will be saved in a file called Exercise11 and stored in the Examples folder you created in Chapter 1, which is, in turn stored in the Windows folder.

5 If you want to save your work onto a floppy disk, insert one into the drive, enter **A:\Exercise11** into **File name:** and click **Save**.

Find and replace

If you click on **Edit** you will see two useful options towards the bottom of the menu list. These are **Find** and **Replace**. Finding and replacing is a way of searching for particular words, characters or phrases and replacing them with others. This is very useful in long documents. In order to use these functions you need a passage to work with – I suggest that you work with the Asimov paragraph you used earlier.

EXERCISE 12

Find and Replace

■ Duration: 15 minutes

1 If you position the cursor at the beginning of the Asimov passage and click on **Find** a window will open asking you to specify what you with to find (**Find what**). Enter a word you wish to find, such as 'books', and click on **Find Next**. The find window will stay on the screen and the word you are seeking will be highlighted (if it's present in the text you're searching). If you click on **Find Next** again, the next time that word appears will be located – and so on.

2 The replace option allows you to both find a word and change it for something else. If you click on **Edit** and **Replace** you need to enter both the word you want to find and the one you want to replace it with. Replace works in the same way as Find.

3 Experiment with finding and replacing words.

Spell checking

If you have doubts about your spelling or simply want to ensure that your letters are free of spelling errors then you will find the spell checker function essential. Spell checking is an automatic method of reviewing your document to identify any possible spelling mistakes and suggesting alternative spellings – however, *you* must choose which is the correct spelling. Sometimes the application gets it wrong – and it won't pick up for you that you've used a wrong word if it's spelt correctly (e.g. 'there' instead of 'their').

EXERCISE 13

Spell checking

■ Duration: 20 minutes

1 Click on **Tools** and select **Spelling and Grammar**. The window shown in Figure 31 will pop up. If you check your Asimov passage the system will identify 'Asimov' as a mistake. If you want to accept the alternative spelling the software suggests, click on **Change**. If you accept the change, the word will be corrected automatically. If you want to refuse the suggestion, click on **Ignore**.

The spell checker will continue to work through the passage. If

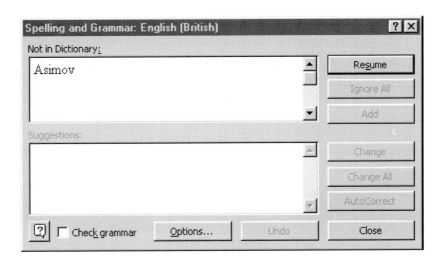

FIGURE 31 *Using the spell checker*

it finds mistakes, it will ask you to **Change** or **Ignore** the suggestion.

2 Asimov is *not* a spelling mistake – it is simply an unusual word. The spell checker is based on a dictionary built into the application. The spell checker will identify any word which is not included in its dictionary as a mistake. It is therefore important for you to check each error to ensure it really *is* a spelling mistake. If you want to add words to the dictionary, click on **Add** (Figure 31) and follow the instructions the computer gives you.

Inserting clip art

Insert clip art is a straightforward way of placing pictures into your documents. This is very useful because you can add considerable interest to your work with a few well placed pictures. Word 97 is supplied with a range of images called **clip art**, which you can use within your documents. Other applications (which we will discuss in Chapter 5) can help you produce your own images. You can also buy collections of clip art.

EXERCISE 14

Inserting pictures

■ Duration: 20 minutes

1 You can insert pictures (**graphics**) into your documents using the Insert Picture function. Position the mouse pointer where you want to place the picture then click on the menu item

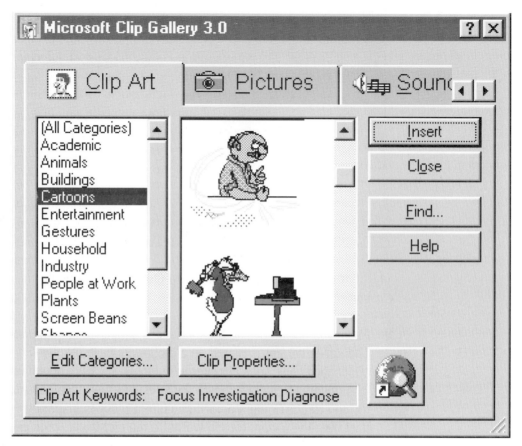

FIGURE 32 *Choosing clip art*

Insert and select **Picture**. Five options will appear. We will concentrate on the top two, **Clip Art** and **From File**. The first provides access to the clip art that is available within Windows, the second allows you to access other images that you have created or bought.

2   Click on **Clip Art**. The window shown in Figure 32 will appear. Windows comes with a small range of images. If you click once on one of the subjects listed in the left-hand column you can preview a number of images in the right-hand window. If you want to insert the picture double-click on the chosen clip.

3   Practise choosing different clip art images, previewing them and placing them into your document.

4   If you want to, save your document as a file. Click on **File** and **Save** and in the box **File name**: enter

C:\Windows\Examples\Exercise14. Click on **Save** and your document will be saved in a file called Exercise14. It is stored in the Examples folder you created in Chapter 1, which is in turn stored in the Windows folder.

5 If you want to save your work on a floppy disk, insert one into the drive, enter **A:\Exercise14** into the **File name:** box and click **Save**.

How do I load an existing file?

■ LOADING FROM THE HARD DISK

You have saved a number of documents in your Examples file. Word allows you to load these files so you can revise them. If you click on **File** and **Open**, a window called Open appears, which looks exactly the same as the Save window. You have two ways of locating your file.

1 The first is to enter the path of the file in the box **File name:** (for example, type **C:\Windows\Examples\ Exercise10**) and click on **Open**.

2 Alternatively, you can explore the hard disk's hierarchy of folders by clicking on the down arrow button next to the **Look in:** until you find Windows and Examples, scrolling down the box below and double-clicking on the file when you find it.

■ LOADING FROM A FLOPPY DISK

If you would like to load a file from a floppy disk, insert the floppy disk into the drive. Click on **File** and **Open**, enter **A:** into the **File name:** box and click on **Open**. A list of the files on the floppy disk will be shown in the scrolling window. To load any of the files you need to double-click on it.

EXERCISE 15

Explore the folders

■ Duration: 15 minutes

1 In Word, click on **File** and **Open**. The Open window will appear – this is similar to the window in Figure 18.

2 Click on the down arrow button next to **Look in:** and a list of folders will appear. Click on **C:** and see if you can locate the Windows folder in the scrolling box below.

3 Double-click on the Windows folder icon and try to locate the Examples folder.

4 Double-click on the Examples folder and you will see a list of files appear in the scrolling box. These should be the files you have saved (for example: Exercise7, Exercise9, Exercise10, Exercise14).

5 Choose one of the files and double-click on it. The file will be loaded into Word.

6 You can change the name of the file by clicking **File** and **Save As**. A window identical to the Save window will appear. Enter a new name by typing **C:\Windows\Examples\Exercise15** (for example) and clicking **Save**. This is a useful way of saving a series of different versions of the same document.

How to print out documents

Printing is a standard function within all Windows applications, so if you know how to print in one Windows application you can do it in all of them.

 Print

 Print Preview

The printing options are available on the toolbar as two icons and as menu options under **File**. If you click on **File** you will locate two functions, **Print Preview** and **Print**. These are also available as icons on the toolbar.

If you click on either of the print preview options then you will see a miniature display of your word-processing page. This will allow you to check the overall layout. When you are finished click on the close button, which is located on the toolbar. If you are not happy with your layout you can change it before you print using the techniques you learnt earlier.

When you are ready to print click on **Print** or on the icon. A display like the one shown in Figure 33 will appear.

As you can see, the print dialog box is divided into several sections:

- the top of the display shows details of the printer connected to the computer
- the area on the middle left-hand side allows you to choose if you want to print all the document, just the current page or particular pages

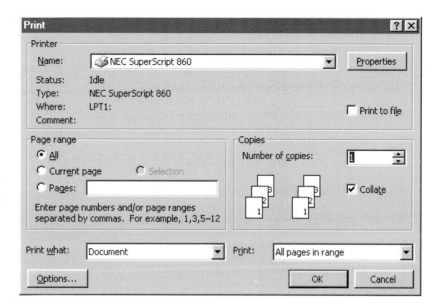

FIGURE 33 *The printing dialog box*

- the area on the middle right-hand side allows you to select how many copies you want to print
- the bottom of the display confirms your decisions. By clicking on the **OK** button you start printing.

What next?

This chapter has introduced you to word processing. It is important to practise your new skills as much as possible. Use your word processor to prepare:

- notes for school
- job applications
- shopping lists
- letters to friends
- business letters

instead of writing them by hand. Take advantage of every opportunity to try out your skills.

SELF TEST QUESTIONS

If you want to test your understanding of this chapter try to answer these questions. The answers are given at the end of the book.

1 What shape does the mouse pointer change into when in the work area of a word processor?

2 What happens when the text reaches the end of a line?

3 How do you create a new line in a document?

4 What facility would you use to change the page layout of your document?

5 Explain what the gutter is.

6 How does text look if you use right justification?

7 Which function allows you to correct errors?

8 Name the two modes of operation of a word processor.

9 What are the sets of pictures you can buy to insert into your document called?

10 What would you use find and replace to do?

Spreadsheets

> ## By the end of this chapter you should be able to:
>
> - Identify the main functions of a spreadsheet
>
> - Create and amend a spreadsheet
>
> - Adapt a spreadsheet (e.g. add and remove columns and rows)
>
> - Efficiently enter information on a spreadsheet
>
> - Use a spreadsheet to carry out calculations
>
> - Change the format of the spreadsheet

Computers are good with numbers. A spreadsheet is an **application** designed to exploit the computer's power to work with numbers. Spreadsheets are useful whenever you need to calculate expenditure, work with tables of data or simply present numerical information. They are widely used in the home, business, school and college.

Spreadsheets are used for a range of different purposes in the home:

- planning family income and expenditure
- producing self-employed accounts
- calculating tax returns
- doing science homework,

in business:

- doing the accounts
- planning projects
- undertaking engineering calculations
- modelling business processes
- presenting numerical information
- calculating invoices,

and in education:

- carrying out scientific investigations
- studying mathematical models
- presenting survey results.

This chapter is divided into three tutorials, which include exercises that will allow you to practise many of the ideas presented in the text.

Tutorial 7 → Introduction

What is a spreadsheet?

Figure 34 shows the main features of Microsoft Excel, a modern spreadsheet used extensively in commercial companies, educational institutions, government offices and the home. Microsoft Excel is a Windows application, so information can be transferred from it to other Windows applications. For example, a Microsoft Word document can be

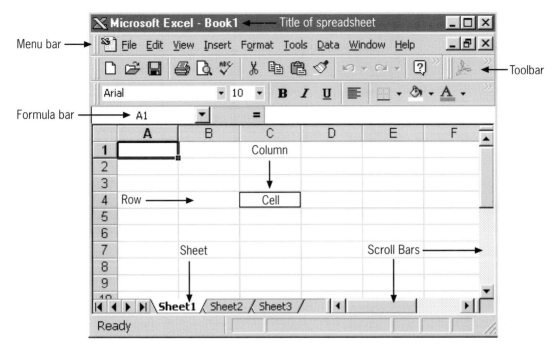

FIGURE 34 *Microsoft Excel*

copied and pasted into a Microsoft Excel sheet by using copy and paste within the two applications. In the same way an Excel sheet can be copied and pasted into Word.

The Microsoft Excel display has three main areas:

1 Menu, toolbar and formula bars, which you can see at the top of Figure 34. These provide you with the controls with which to develop your sheet. Notice the similarities with the Word's controls (see Figure 18) such as font, character size, bold, italics and underline.

2 Work area. This area is divided into rows and columns (see Figures 34 and 35). The sheet is often larger than the display and you move it around using the horizontal and vertical scroll bars.

3 The status line. By displaying 'Ready' this tells you the sheet is waiting for you to begin work.

How do spreadsheets work?

All spreadsheets work in the same basic way. Information is presented in a large table, which is divided into **rows** and

	A	B	C	D	E
1	Expenditure				
2			January	February	March
3	Mortgage		340.56	340.56	340.56
4	Electricity		120.00		
5	Gas		70.00		
6	Travel		56.00	45.50	78.90
7					
8	Total		586.56	386.06	419.46

FIGURE 35 *A simple spreadsheet*

columns. This is called a **sheet**. The rows are numbered and the columns labelled with a letter. Figure 35 shows a simple spreadsheet.

The sheet is divided by a pattern of rows and columns into many **cells**. Each cell has a single unique name, provided by combining the column letter and the row number (e.g. A1, B7, C4).

In any cell it is possible to place a phrase, a number or a **formula**. For example, a formula would total the figures in a whole column or a whole row. In Figure 35, cell C8 has the following formula:

$$C8 = C3 + C4 + C5 + C6$$
$$586.56 = 340.56 + 120 + 70 + 56$$

Mathematical formulae are used to carry out calculations. Once you have developed your sheet, every time you change a figure, the total will automatically be updated. This is a useful feature of spreadsheets.

EXERCISE 16

Explore Excel

■ Duration: 60 minutes

1 Double-click on the Excel icon and the software will load (a small hourglass appears alongside the mouse pointer to show you that something is happening inside the computer).

2 A screen appears for a moment or two telling you that you have loaded Microsoft Excel 97 but is rapidly displaced by the Excel screen. This may occupy the whole, or only part of, the display

screen. If it occupies only part of the screen (i.e. it is in a window) then click the maximise button (top right-hand corner of the Microsoft Excel window; see Figure 34). The spreadsheet display should now fill the screen.

3 In the work area you will notice that one cell is highlighted (usually A1 – top left-hand corner of the work area). This is the cell in which the application is expecting you to enter data. You can change the cell by clicking on another cell or by pressing the arrow keys. If you move the mouse over the work area you will notice that the pointer changes shape from an arrow to a + bar. If you move the mouse over the menu, toolbar or status areas it turns back into an arrow. If you click on a cell an I beam will appear in the cell to indicate that this is where your text will appear when you enter it.

Highlight a different cell by using the mouse and the arrow keys. If the arrow keys that form part of the number pad do not seem to work, you probably have the numbers lock (Num Lock) key pressed. When this key is pressed, the computer only recognises the key to represent a number (2, 4, 6, 8, etc.). Press the key once and it will be cancelled. The numbers lock is often shown to be on by a light on the keyboard. It is off when the light is not illuminated.

4 Enter the data given in Figure 36.

5 Look at the toolbar and observe what it tells you about the font and size of character you are using (see Figure 34). You can change the font and character size of an entry by clicking on the cell – the cell will be outlined in a thick black line to show that it has been selected. If you change the font, size or style (bold, italics or underline) then the characters in the cell will also change. For example:

January – Bembo size 10

January – Times New Roman size 10 italics

January – Times New Roman size 12 bold and underlined

6 If you want to change an area larger than a single cell then press and hold down the left mouse button, drag the pointer over the area you want to change and release the button. The area you have selected is highlighted in black. If you change

	A	B	C	D	E	F	G
1							
2	Item		January	April	July	October	Total
3							
4	Telephone		150	150	150	150	600
5	Insurance		15	15	15	15	60
6	Rent		300	300	300	300	1200
7	Council Tax		220	220	220	220	880
8							
9	Total		665	665	665	665	2740
10							

FIGURE 36 *Table of data for Exercise 16*

your mind, simply click the mouse with the pointer outside of your chosen area and the highlighting will be removed. Try to highlight the whole of the table you have just entered.

With the table highlighted change the character size to 16. You will see the table change – the size of the cells will increase to accommodate the new characters. Try making some of the characters bold, change the titles to be in italics and choose a new font.

Practise the highlighting technique until you are confident. Highlighting is used extensively to edit tables.

7 Excel 97 allows you to insert extra rows and columns into a table. Try inserting an extra column between two of your columns (e.g. between January and April). To do this, click the pointer on the April column (the cell will be highlighted), click on **Insert** and then on **Columns**. A new column will be placed to the left of the chosen column.

Try inserting an extra row above the 'Total' line. Click on any entry in that line. Click on **Insert** and then **Rows**. A new row will be inserted above 'Total'.

Experiment with adding rows and columns to the table. If you make a mistake, use Undo to correct it. The Undo option is located in the **Edit** menu or as an icon on the toolbar. The Undo and Redo icons are shown in Figure 37.

These icons also appear on the Word 97 and Access 97

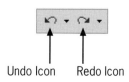

Undo Icon   Redo Icon

FIGURE 37 *Undo and redo icons*

toolbars and serve the same function – they undo your last action. As in Word, you can use undo repeatedly to correct a series of steps. The redo option, which appears as soon as you have used undo once, is equally useful. The two choices allow you to correct mistakes easily.

8 Explore the options available under the different menu items (e.g. **File**, **Edit** and **View**). See if you can locate:

- new
- open
- save
- print
- cut
- copy
- paste
- spelling
- sort.

These are some of the useful functions which spreadsheets provide. You should expect to find these features in all spreadsheets, but not necessarily under the same menu items. Compare the layout in Excel with what you identified while exploring Word. You should notice many similarities.

9 If you rest your mouse pointer over the toolbar without clicking a small message will appear to explain what the button does. See if you can find the following:

- new
- open
- print
- spelling
- cut
- copy
- paste
- sort.

You may have noticed that some of the toolbar items are duplicated under a menu. This is normal in almost all programs. There is no right way. *You* choose the way that *you* prefer. The icons are often identical to those you should have found when you were exploring Word, if they serve the same function (such as opening a file, cut, paste and redo). This is because they are all Windows applications.

10 Save your document as a file. This process is the same for all Windows applications – the procedure you follow to save a spreadsheet file is exactly the same as the one you used to save a word-processing file. If you click on **File** and **Save** a window opens (look back to Figure 18). In the box **File name:** enter **C:\Windows\Examples\Exercise16** (remember to click in the box to allow you to enter text) and then click on the **Save** button (right side of window). Your document will be saved as a file called Exercise16 and it will be stored in the Examples folder you created in Chapter 1, which is in turn stored in the Windows folder.

11 If you want to save your work onto a floppy disk, insert a floppy into the drive, enter **A:\Exercise16** in **File name:** and click **Save**.

| Tutorial 8 | → | Getting started |

When you first load Excel 97, the working area is divided into rows and columns. The cell in the top left-hand corner is highlighted and the formula bar reads A1. This shows that cell A1 is currently ready for data to be entered. Whatever you enter into the cell will be repeated on the formula bar after the equals sign (=). Information typed into the spreadsheet will always appear in the highlighted cell. To change cells simply click on the new cell with the mouse pointer. The name of the new cell will be shown on the formula bar (C8, D5, etc.).

On the top of the display you will see the name of the spreadsheet. When you first load the application, the program gives the spreadsheet a temporary name – Book1. You can change this name later when you save the sheet.

EXERCISE 17

Creating a spreadsheet

■ Duration: 1 hour

1 Enter the title of the spreadsheet – Analysis of Car Prices – starting in cell B2. You will notice that the text flows over the next cell (B3).

2 Insert the table of information given in Figure 38.

You will notice that letters and numbers position themselves at

	A	B	C	D	E	F	G	H
4	Manufacturer		Model		Engine	Registration		Price
5								
6	Fiat		Uno 45		999	E		495
7	Ford		Fiesta		1000	F		1657
8	Vauxhall		Astra		1800	H		3150
9	Peugeot		405GT		1800	H		3995
10	Vauxhall		Astra		1800	H		3495
11	Ford		Escort		1800	H		3795
12	Ford		Fiesta		1000	F		1495
13	Vauxhall		Carlton		1800	B		650
14	Peugeot		309		1300	D		550
15	Ford		Fiesta		1100	F		1795
16	Ford		Sierra		1800	B		2995
17	Renault		Saframe		3000	L		4995
18	Fiat		Tipo		1600	K		2195

Sheet1 / Sheet2 / Sheet3 /

FIGURE 38 *Spreadsheet for Exercise 17*

different sides of the cell. Numbers always move to the right and letters to the left.

3 You are going to use this spreadsheet again so you need to save it to disk. Click on **File** and then **Save**. If this is the first time you have saved your file you will asked to name the file, and you have the option to choose the type of file you want to save as (for Excel, the type of file will be Microsoft Excel Workbook). Enter **C:\Windows\Examples\Exercise17** in the File name: box to save the file in the Examples folder within the Windows folder. After you have saved the file for the first time, every time you press **Save** the computer automatically updates the file without asking you to name it or choose its type. The file name will appear on top of the Excel display.

4 If you want to save your work to a floppy disk then insert a disk into the drive, enter **A:\Exercise17** under **File name:** and click on **Save**.

Filling in your sheet

There are several ways of adding information to a spreadsheet. The obvious way is to simply enter your data from the keyboard, using the mouse or arrow keys to change cells. There are several other ways, including copying and pasting in much the same way as you copy and paste text in Word. The process you use to copy or cut out an area of your sheet and paste it into another part of the sheet is exactly the same as you used with Word. You need to highlight the area by holding down the left-hand mouse button, dragging the pointer over your chosen area and then releasing the button. You can then click on **Edit** and then **Copy** or **Cut.** An alternative way is to use the icons on the bar (e.g. scissors mean cut). Another method is to use the fill handle (Figure 39), a small

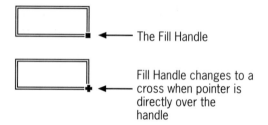

FIGURE 39 *Using the fill handle*

square you will see at the bottom right-hand corner of each cell. If you position your mouse pointer over the fill handle the pointer turns into a cross (**+**). Hold down the left mouse button and drag the cell. The content of the original cell is copied into the cell over which it has been dragged.

If you are copying a sequence, such as the days of the week or the months of the year, then the spreadsheet attempts to guess the next items in the sequence. For example:

January	February			

January and February have been entered from the keyboard. If the cell is now dragged over the next three cells, the spreadsheet will guess the next items in the series so that March, April and May are filled in.

January	February	March	April	May

This will work for any series, so that the spreadsheet could predict, say, all the days of the week (Monday, Tuesday, Wednesday, etc) after just a few have been entered.

Using a spreadsheet to do calculations

Probably the most useful feature of a spreadsheet is its ability to calculate. It allows you to set up a range of standard calculations so that all you have to do is fill in the raw data and the spreadsheet turns it into meaningful results. You can establish a spreadsheet to work out your tax, review your household expenditure or calculate your profits if you are self-employed, and it will continue to work as long as you are able to fill in the new figures. The difficult part is to design the formulae that perform the calculations.

The arithmetic symbols used on a computer are slightly different from the ones you use on paper:

+   add
−   subtract
/   divide
*   multiply.

So, for example,

C8*10   means multiply the contents of cell C8 by 10
C8*E4   means multiply the contents of cell C8 by the contents of cell E4
A9/2   means divide the contents of cell A9 by 2
A9/F1   means divide the contents of cell A9 by the contents of cell F1
H12+B2   means add the contents of cell H12 to the contents of cell B2
D3-F23   means subtract the contents of cell F23 from the contents of D3

It is possible to use quite complex formulae. For example:

C8*10/V4+H2-W14 means multiply the contents of cell C8 by 10, then divide the answer by the contents of cell V4, and then add the result of subtracting the contents of cell W14 from the contents of cell H2.

When you have a formula which is composed of several arithmetic operators (e.g. add and multiply), Excel works

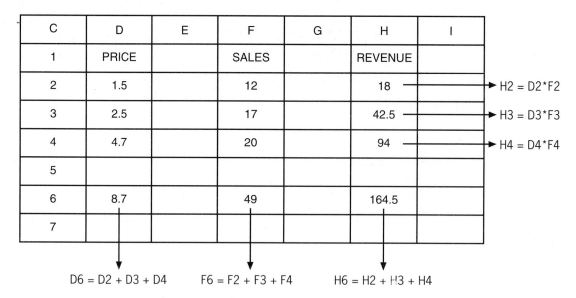

FIGURE 40 *Example formulae*

them out according to a standard rule. It will work out multiplication and division first and addition and subtraction second. If the formula contains multiplication and division it works out the calculation from left to right. Some examples of formulae are shown in Figure 40.

When you have finished entering your formula in order to make it calculate, you need to click on the equals sign (=) in the formula bar. A Window will appear to explain the calculation and when you click on OK to close the window you will see the value appear on the spreadsheet.

Microsoft Excel comes with a number of standard functions that help you make more complex calculations. These include:

■ Average(range) – works out the average in the range (e.g. Average(D2:D4) = 2.9)

■ Count(range) – works out the number of items in the range (e.g. Count(D2:D4) = 3)

■ Max(range) – inserts the highest value in the range (e.g. Max(D2:D4) = 4.7)

■ Min(range) – inserts the lowest value in the range (e.g. Min(D2:D4) = 1.5)

■ SUM(range) – totals the figures in the range (e.g. SUM(D2:D4) = 8.7).

To use the standard features enter them into the appropriate cell.

The SUM function is also available on the toolbar, where, if you click on the sigma icon (Σ), it will insert a SUM function into the cell which is highlighted. This will sum the contents of the column of figures above the SUM.

EXERCISE 18

Work out the formulae

■ Duration: 1 hour

1　Load the spreadsheet that you saved in the last exercise.

2　Enter the formulae that you would use to calculate the total of the car prices, average car price, maximum price of a car and the minimum price of a car.

The total cost is 31452 (SUM the contents of column H, Price)
The average price is 2419.3 (divide the SUM of column H by the total number of entries COUNT (range))
The maximum price is 4995 (Use MAX(range) function on column H)
The minimum price is 495 (Use MIN(range) function on column H)

3　Don't forget to click on the equals sign on the formula bar to signal the formulae to calculate their results.

4　Once you have sorted out the formulae, experiment with changing the car prices and see what happens.

5　Once you feel confident, save the file. This will save the changes you have made to the spreadsheet.

Tutorial 9 → **What else can you do with a spreadsheet?**

Microsoft Excel provides you with a comprehensive application which has a wide range of features. Some of the other features that you may find useful are:

■ formatting
■ sorting
■ changing styles.

Changing the format of spreadsheet data

A very important formatting feature is the ability to change the format of the numbers in the spreadsheet (e.g. increase and decrease the number of decimal places). Figure 41 shows five ways of changing the style of spreadsheet numbers using icons which appear on the toolbar.

EXERCISE 19

Changing the numbers

■ Duration: 30 minutes

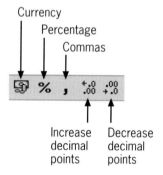

FIGURE 41 *Formatting number styles*

1 In a blank sheet enter the following numbers: 100.00, 1000.00, 10000.00, 100000, 123.23.

2 Systematically highlight the numbers, choose one of the number styles from the toolbar and see what effect it has on the numbers. You should see:

■ a pound sign appear when you choose the currency option
■ a percentage sign will appear when you choose the % option
■ commas inserted in the appropriate places (e.g. 100,000.00)
■ the number of decimal points increase and decrease as you click on the options (e.g. 1000.0000 or 123.2).

3 Continue to experiment until you are confident that you can predict the changes that will occur when you choose an option.

How do you change the overall format of the spreadsheet?

If you investigate the **Format** menu you will discover a choice called **Autoformat**. If you click on this item the display shown in Figure 42 will appear. This provides you with a range of styles to chose from (e.g. simple) and a preview window so that you can see the effect of the style.

EXERCISE 20

Different styles

■ Duration: 30 minutes

1 Investigate the different styles available to you through the **Autoformat** option.

2 Try out each style (from Simple to 3D Effects 2) and watch the preview display to see what changes.

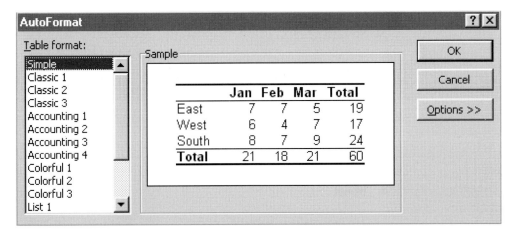

FIGURE 42 *Using Autoformat*

Sorting data

Microsoft Excel provides you with two ways of sorting your information – you will find these on the tool bar. Figure 43 shows you the two icons. The **AZ** icon will sort your data from highest to lowest value, while the **ZA** icon will sort them from lowest to highest. Highlight your list and then click on the appropriate icon.

Changing the overall characteristics of a

spreadsheet

You will probably have noticed that some of the titles you use are longer than the width of a cell. This can make your sheets appear untidy and amateurish and could be a problem if you are using, say, a spreadsheet of your self-employed earnings to

A to Z sorting	Z to A sorting
100.000.000	100.000
10,000.000	123.230
1,000.000	1,000.000
123.230	10,000.000
100.000	100.000.000

FIGURE 43 *Sorting data*

persuade the bank manager to increase your overdraft. Appearances are often important. Microsoft Excel provides you with many features that allow you to change the layout and appearance of your sheet.

If you click on **Format** then you will be presented with a series of options. The top four are:

- **Cell**
- **Row**
- **Column** and
- **Sheet**.

There are other options but for the moment they are not important. If you click on any of the first four you will be offered still more choices.

Cell provides you with many powerful tools for amending your sheet. Figure 44 shows the choice.

These tools allow you to change the style of the numbers in a similar way to the buttons on the toolbar. You can alter the alignment of your text, change fonts (just as you can from the toolbar buttons), add a border and add colour to your

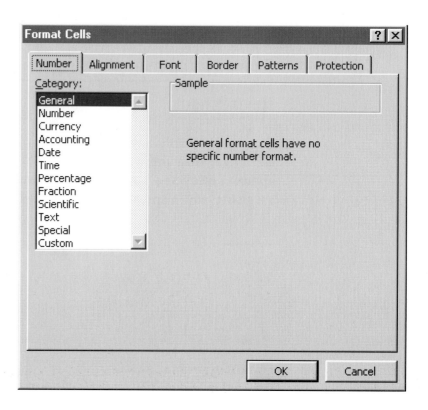

FIGURE 44 *Cell characteristic tools*

sheet. Almost all of these tools are duplicated on the toolbar or within other options in the menu bar. Remember, there are no right ways of making a change: *you* pick the way that suits *you* best.

The other options under **Format** also lead you to more choices. However, for the moment we will concentrate on:

Row – Height

which allows you to change the height of a row,

Column – Width

which allows you to alter the width of a column,

Sheet – Rename

which lets you save your sheet under a new name, and

Sheet – Background

which you use to add a background to your sheet to improve its appearance.

EXERCISE 21

Customising a spreadsheet

■ Duration: 45 minutes

1   Load the spreadsheet you saved in Exercise 18 (the file is called Exercise17).

2   Experiment with the different tools. Remember that you need to highlight a row, column or area before you can change it.

3   Explore the options – if you get into a mess just use the undo option until you get back to a display you are happy with.

What next?

You should now feel confident about the basic functions of creating and amending a spreadsheet. It is important that you attempt to create a spreadsheet of your own. Identify a sheet which could be useful (such as your home expenditure), develop an outline on paper and then attempt to transfer it to Excel. Concentrate initially on getting the information into the sheet with formulae to calculate totals and so on. Once you have a functioning spreadsheet try to improve its appearance by adding blank rows and columns, changing heights and widths until it looks good.

SELF TEST QUESTIONS

If you want to test your understanding of this chapter try to answer these questions. The answers are given at the end of the book.

1   What are the three component parts of a spreadsheet?

2   What shape does the mouse pointer change to when moved across the work area?

3   What do you use to copy a cell's content to other cells in the row or column?

4   On a computer, which symbol is used for multiplication?

5   Write down the formula you would use to divide the contents of cell C8 by the contents of cell M11.

6   How do you increase and decrease the number of decimal places in a cell?

7   How can you change the overall format of a spreadsheet?

8   How do you sort your information into ascending or descending order?

9   How would you indicate to Microsoft Excel which part of a spreadsheet you wish to change?

10 In what areas (e.g. colleges) are spreadsheets used?

Databases

By the end of this chapter you should be able to:

- Identify the main functions of Microsoft Access

- Create a straightforward table

- Understand the nature of a field, a record and a table

- Understand the various data types that can be stored in a database

- Question the information stored in a database

- Use a Wizard to create a table and a database

We are all surrounded by many different databases but often are unaware of their existence. However, almost all your interactions with companies, local authorities and government involves information you provide being stored on a computer in some type of database. When you visit the library, telephone the bank or pay a bill, your records are held on a database. If you read forms carefully you will often see that they ask your permission to store your details electronically. This means that your records are being held on a database.

A database is a means of storing information on a computer so that it can be searched, analysed, amended and manipulated quickly and efficiently. In many ways it serves the same purpose as an office filing cabinet full of files that are organised alphabetically. If the office staff wanted to find some information they would search the cabinet for the correct folder and then read its contents. To help them find the information a company might design standard forms on which to record your information. The staff will then know to look for a particular form because it will contain the information they require.

This type of paper database works well within limits. You could not change the filing system (e.g. from alphabetical to date of birth) without a lot of effort, it would take a significant amount of time to find requested information – and if someone else had removed the folder you might never find it. An electronic database allows you to search for information by a wide range of characteristics. With a computer you are not restricted to only one filing system, it takes only a few seconds to locate any record and many users can work on the same information at the same time.

Microsoft Access 97 is a database **application program** which helps you to build databases. You can buy ready-prepared blank databases, which allow you to keep one type of information in them (e.g. a stamp collection database) but you cannot change the design of this type of database to suit another type of information. Microsoft Access 97 is different in that it allows you to design, create and change as many different databases as you like. The design and creation of databases is a complex and specialised task, and this chapter will provide you with only an introduction to the subject.

Most computer users rarely design and create databases; most will use databases created by other people. Developing an understanding of how they are constructed will help you to become an efficient user.

The chapter is divided into three tutorials, which include exercises that will allow you to practise many of the ideas presented in the text.

Tutorial 10 → Introduction to Access 97

How do you load Microsoft Access 97?

Access is loaded in the same way as many other applications that work in the Windows environment. You can double-click on the icon on the desktop or use the program menu, which you locate by clicking on the Start button, highlighting Program and searching the list for the Access item.

A window initially appears (Figure 45), which asks you whether you want to create a new database using a blank database or a database Wizard, or whether you want to open an existing database. A list of existing databases is shown in

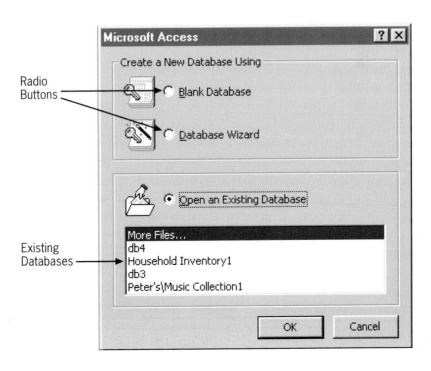

FIGURE 45 *Microsoft Access 97 initial dialog window*

the window. You can open one by double-clicking on it. To create a new database click once on the radio button of your choice and then on **OK**.

What is a blank database?

A blank database is rather like an empty filing cabinet. All the files are in alphabetical order but no one has put any papers into the folders. By creating a blank database you can develop a customised database to precisely meet your needs. However, it does mean you must make a number of choices and decisions about the nature and structure of your database. You must have a good understanding of the type of information you want to store and how you want to use it.

If you choose to produce a blank database you will be asked to give it a name and then the screen shown in Figure 46 will appear. This illustrates the component parts (or

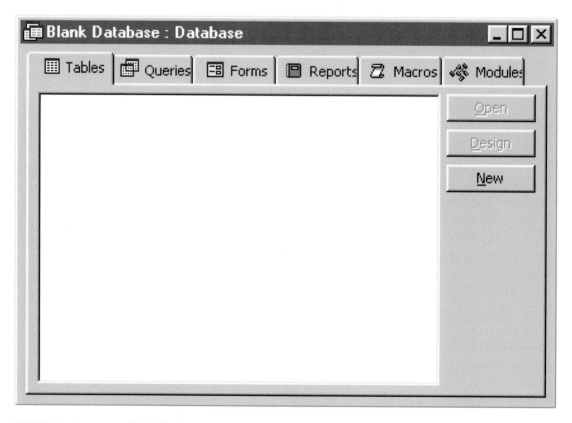

FIGURE 46 *Creating a blank database*

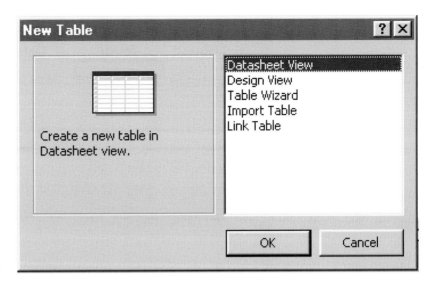

FIGURE 47 *A blank table*

objects) of an Access database. These are tables, queries, forms, reports, macros and modules. All these parts are known as **objects** within Access. During this tutorial we will concentrate on tables because these are where you store your information within a database. Access is a **relational database**. Most modern databases are relational, which means that related information is stored in one place (a table).

Before you can add information to the blank database you need to design the table in which it will be stored. If you click on **Tables** and then on **New**, a blank table will appear (Figure 47).

This screen again presents a number of options to choose from. At this stage click once on **Datasheet View** and then on **OK** – the screen in Figure 48 will appear, showing you a blank **datasheet**. This is similar to a spreadsheet and operates in a similar way. You can enter numbers, text and other information but it will not perform calculations for you. The datasheet provides you with examples of two of the main structures of all databases. These are **fields** and **records**. A field is an individual item of data (e.g. surname) while a record is a group of fields which make up an entire piece of information (e.g. name and address).

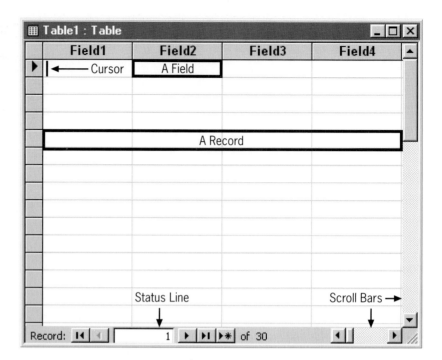

FIGURE 48 *Datasheet view of a blank table*

EXERCISE 22

Creating a table

■ Duration: 1 hour

1 Load Microsoft Access and select to create a new blank database by clicking on the radio button and then **OK**. You will be asked to name your database; when you have finished, click on the **OK** button. The display shown in Figure 46 will appear. Click on **New** to indicate you are going to produce a new table. Figure 47 will appear – choose **Datasheet View** and click on **OK**. Figure 48 will now appear showing a blank datasheet.

2 You are going to produce a database of names and addresses (an electronic address book). The first step is to enter some information. Enter the six names and addresses given below into the datasheet using the tab key or by clicking on the field with mouse pointer to change fields. When you start to enter the information a pen will appear at the beginning of the record line to show you which row you are working on. Figure 49 shows a completed table.

Mr John Brown, 12 St Andrew Street, Glasgow, GE2 5RJ
Miss Ruth King, 245 Lloyd Avenue, York, YO1 7UY
Dr Singh, 27 Violet Road, Sheffield, S10 4EH

Table1 : Table					
Title	**First Name**	**Last Name**	**Number**	**Street**	**Town**
Mr	John	Brown	12	St Andrew St	Glasgow
Miss	Ruth	King	245	Lloyd Avenue	York
Dr		Singh	27	Violet Road	Sheffield
Mr	Christopher	Burger	67	Hillcrest Road	Birmingham
Miss	Jane	Dean	89	Somerset Lane	Chesterfield
Mr	William	Blink	456	Long Street	London

FIGURE 49 *Completed table*

Mr Christopher Burger, 67 Hillcrest Road, Birmingham, B34 9HJ

Miss Jane Dean, 89 Somerset Lane, Chesterfield, C23 8GH

Mr William Blink, 456 Long Street, London, L12 5TG

3 Note that the field names in Figure 49 are not the same as you would see at first. When you first open a new table the fields are named field 1, field 2 etc. Change the field names by clicking anywhere in the field column and then on **Format** and **Rename Column**. Enter the new field names.

What is a Wizard?

Many Windows 95 applications use a **Wizard**. This allows you to perform many complex tasks easily by choosing between options. Microsoft has a number of Wizards, including a **Table Wizard**, which helps you to design tables for your database. Many databases need several tables which would require a great deal of time to create by hand. The wizard allows you to produce them quickly and effectively.

■ USING TABLE WIZARD

Access the **Table Wizard** by:

1 Choosing to create a new blank database

2 Naming your new database

3 Clicking on the Table tab (see Figure 46) and **New**

4 Selecting the **Table Wizard** from the list in Figure 47 and clicking on **OK**

5 Figure 50 will appear, to show you have accessed the Wizard.

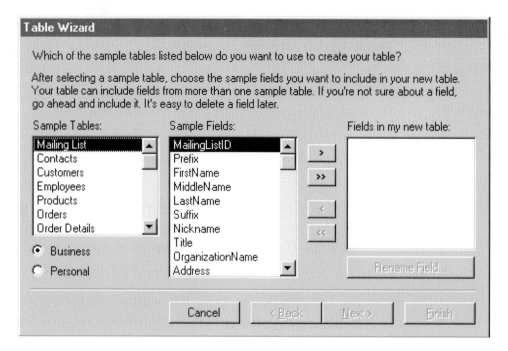

FIGURE 50 *Table Wizard dialog box*

Table Wizard gives two sets of options that are shown by two radio buttons (**Business** and **Personal**). The business option provides you with a selection of business tables and their associated fields while the personal one offers a selection of personally oriented tables. Select a table by clicking on it so that it is highlighted and then double-click on the fields, which will make up the tables. You can add and remove fields from any of the tables using the arrow buttons. When you are finished click on **Next**. You will be asked to confirm the name of your table and if you want a **primary key** to be established for the table. A primary key is a unique identifier for each record, which Access will create for you automatically or which you can prepare manually. It is useful because it helps the database to find each record.

EXERCISE 23

Using Table Wizard

■ Duration: 1 hour

1   See if you can create the table in Figure 51 using the **Table Wizard**.

2   Explore the different options and see what you can discover. When you have created a new table the wizard will tell you if it

Plants : Table				_ □
Plant ID	Common Nam	Genus	Light Preferen	Watering Frequency
▶ (AutoNumber)				

FIGURE 51 *Example table for Exercise 23*

is related to any of the existing tables in the database. As you are only practising you are likely to be told that the tables are not related.

3 Carry on until you are a confident user of the **Table Wizard**.

What are relationships?

Relational databases keep all their related information in one place, normally a table. However, tables are often inter-related by having one field which relates to all the fields in another table. For example, information on individuals might be kept in two tables, which are related by both being for a named individual:

Table 1: Name and address of individuals
Table 2: Age, gender, weight and height of each individual

When you are constructing a database you need to define the relationships using Access. In our example this is done by telling Access that all the records in table 2 relate to field 1 (Name) in table 1. For example:

Table 1 Record 1 Field 1 is Williams

All the fields in record 1 of table 2 relate to Williams – he is 24 years old, male, weighs 13 st 8 lbs and is 6 ft tall.

These relationships are very important in that they allow the database to link different pieces of information. It could be used to search our example database for men aged 24 and would locate Williams. If the database had not been told the tables were related it could not have located this information.

| Tutorial 11 | → | Data |

What can you store in a field?

When you are developing a database table you will need to tell Access what sort of information each field will hold. The data is defined as a number of standard types:

- text – letters and numbers
- memo – sentences and paragraphs
- numbers – 1, 2, 3, etc.
- date/time – for example, 10 August, 20.00 p.m.
- currency – such as £100
- autonumber – unique values produced by Access which form the primary key
- yes/no – these are called Boolean values
- OLE objects – pictures, graphs, Word files, video, sounds etc.

Access automatically allocates each field a data type. These all require different amounts of memory – yes/no needs only 1 **bit** (8 bits = 1 **byte**) while a picture will need thousands or even millions of bytes.

There is a special data type, a **hyperlink**, that allows you to link the database to other computer resources. These can be on your individual computer, another machine on a network or a World Wide Web (**Internet**) site. You need to be able to describe the location of the resources (e.g. the path name on a computer or the URL for Internet resources).

The area that was blank in Figure 46 will now display a list of the tables you will have created during your exploration of the **Table Wizard**. If you select one of the tables and then click on **Design** you will see the data types of the fields in that table. Access has automatically worked out the data type and in most cases you will not need to change it. However, you can make changes using this display window if you want to.

EXERCISE 24

Data types

■ Duration: 30 minutes

1 Select one of the tables you created during the earlier exercises and click on the **Design** button. The display shown in Figure 52 will appear.

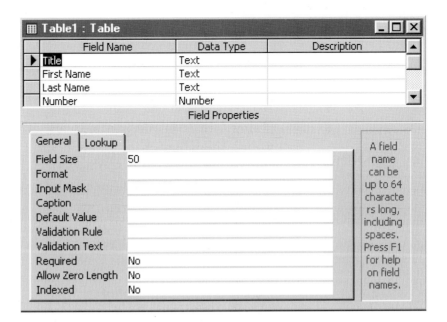

FIGURE 52 *Data types*

2 This figure shows you the data types of the fields of your chosen table. It provides you with a description of each data type which gives you precise details of the data. For example, a text field can hold a maximum of only 256 characters (Figure 52). You can set a text field for any size up to 256 characters manually – or Access will do it automatically for you. The text field in Figure 52 has been set by Access to 50 characters.

3 Explore the different field data types and read the descriptions provided to show you the limits of the field (number of characters, range of numbers, etc.).

4 Continue until you are reasonably sure you know the different types of data.

How do you use a database?

A database is more than just a place to store information – you can ask questions of a large volume of data. If a business had a database of customers who had all bought at least one item then it would be perfectly possible to discover many useful pieces of information, such as:

- where most customers live so that delivery services could be optimised
- what products sell best
- how often customers buy products
- what months have the highest sales.

Access provides you with a range of methods for asking questions and displaying answers. You can simply scroll through the tables of information and extract the information manually or use more sophisticated approaches. The main methods are Find, Sort, Query and Report.

■ FIND

Find will locate a particular record and operates in a similar way to the **Find** facility in Word.

■ SORT

This allows you to change the order of your records by a particular field so that the records are shown in ascending or descending order. This is similar to sorting a spreadsheet by columns.

■ QUERY

With Query you can develop a more complex sort involving more than one table of data. This requires an understanding of the structure and content of the tables. Once you have designed a query it is good practice to save it so that it can be re-used.

■ REPORT

Often you will want information, which results from a query, sort or a set of queries, to be displayed or printed in a form which is easy to understand. Access has the tools for designing a report form to show the results of your questions. To help with this process Access provides you with a **Report Wizard** which lets you design reports by selecting various options.

| **EXERCISE 25**

Northwind

■ Duration: 1 hour | 1 Access is accompanied by a sample database called Northwind, which allows you to explore a finished system. This may be one of the databases listed on the opening screen (Figure 45); if it is, start it up simply by double-clicking on it. If it is not on the list then it can be found by using the find function, which is located in the **Start** button. **Find** is a very useful |

function when you cannot remember where a file is. If you click on **Start**, **Find**, **Files** or **Folders** then a dialog box will appear. To locate this database, enter Northwind into the box called **Named:** and click on **Find Now**. The function will then search the hard disk to locate Northwind. Eventually the database will be found (e.g. **NorthWind C:\Program Files\Microsoft Office\Office\Sample**). To access it, double-click on the icon at the start of the line. This will start up Northwind within Access.

2   The opening screen has an **OK** button which, when you click it, will open up the main part of the database as shown in Figure 53. This shows you the different tables that make up Northwind.

3   Investigate the database by systematically exploring the queries, reports and design for each table. Take notes as you

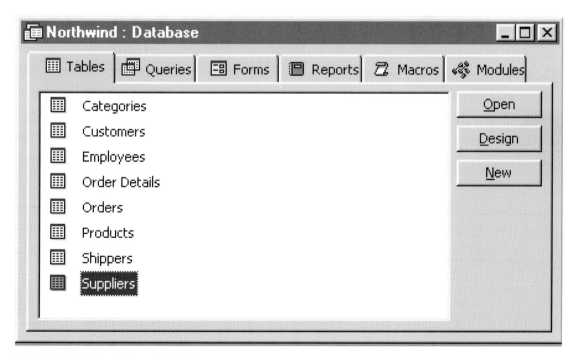

FIGURE 53 *Northwind's main display*

work through the structure. Try to see the relationships between the different tables, identify the different data types, read through the information stored on each table and try to familiarise yourself with the database.

4   You can move between the different options by clicking on the tabs. Double-clicking on the various tables, queries and reports will open them up for you to inspect.

5   Take your time and investigate carefully and systematically.

6   Continue until you are aware of the different elements that make up Northwind.

Tutorial 12 → Creating a database

The straightforward way – using Database Wizard

The individual objects that make up an Access database each have a Wizard to help you produce tables, queries, reports etc. There is also an overall **Database Wizard**, which allows you to select from a variety of options to develop an entire database. For the new or occasional user this is the easiest way of creating a database. It does assume nevertheless that you have a basic understanding of the Access objects.

In the opening Access display (Figure 45) you have the option to select **Database Wizard** by clicking on the radio button and then **OK**. This opens up the window shown in Figure 54.

Database Wizard contains a wide range of databases to choose from (e.g. Music Collections, Expenses and Asset Tracking). Each gives you a customised database for a particular purpose, such as keeping track of your music collection. The wizard will allow you to select from a variety of options to further customise the database to match your needs.

The first step is to select a database by double-clicking on your choice. You will be asked to name your database in exactly the same way as when you created a blank database. From that point you will be given choices (which are explained) and you will need to make selections. One of the

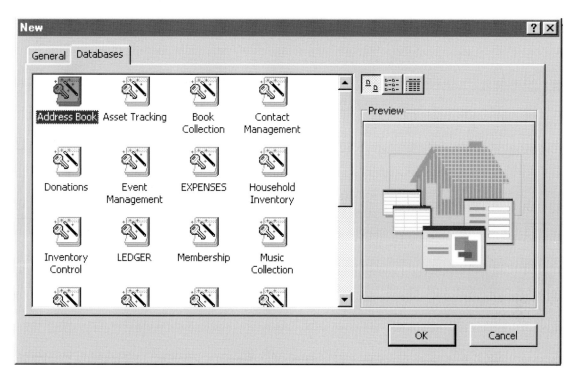

FIGURE 54 *Database Wizard*

most important choices is whether to select extra fields to be included in the tables. This is illustrated in Figure 55. You can opt to include sample data, which may help you learn how to use the database. The databases vary in complexity – some are based on a single table while others have many tables.

When you are ready, click on the **Next** button, which will take you through a series of windows. Each window will ask you to make choices from a series of options. In each case Access will provide you with a default choice if you are not sure what to choose. When you have completed all the choices you will arrive at a window with the **Next** button **greyed out** (i.e. not available); you then need to click on **Finish**. This will create the database. You can watch the process on the screen, which will be completed by the creation of an opening screen display called a switchboard. This provides a friendly entrance to the database (Figure 56). The switchboard allows you to use all the different elements of your database.

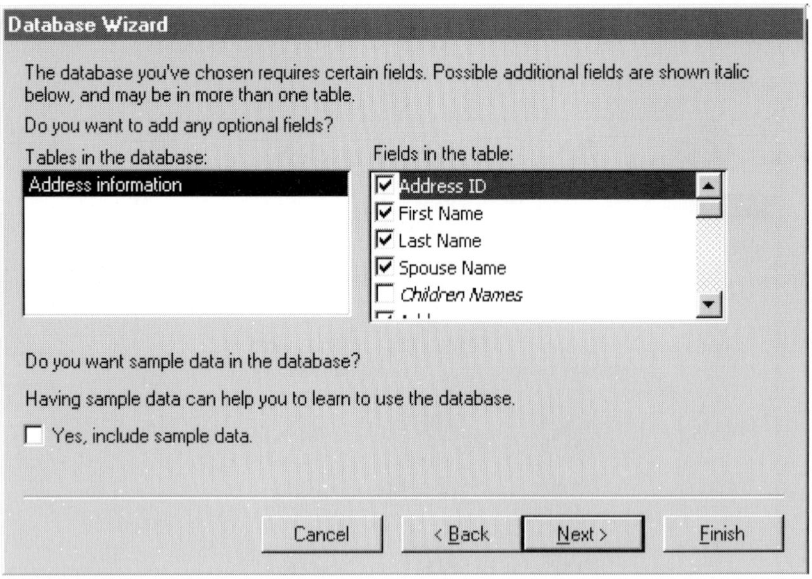

Database Wizard
The database you've chosen requires certain fields. Possible additional fields are shown italic below, and may be in more than one table.
Do you want to add any optional fields?
Tables in the database:
Address information
Fields in the table:
Address ID
First Name
Last Name
Spouse Name
Children Names
Do you want sample data in the database?
Having sample data can help you to learn to use the database.
Yes, include sample data.
Cancel
< Back
Next >
Finish

FIGURE 55 *Adding optional fields*

Main Switchboard
Address Book
Enter/View Addresses
Preview Reports...
Change Switchboard Items
Exit this database

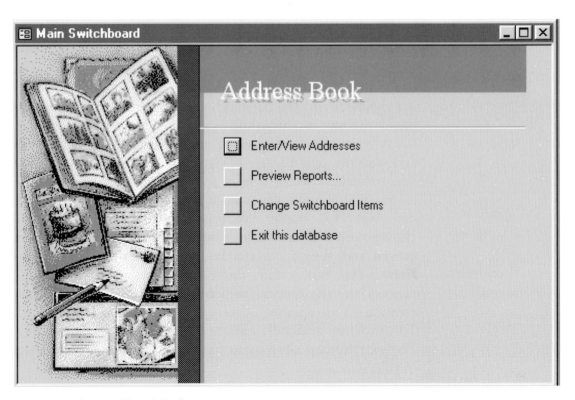

FIGURE 56 *The switchboard display*

EXERCISE 26

Database Wizard

■ Duration: 1 hour

1 Create a database of your own choice using **Database Wizard**.

2 Work through the options and customise your database by adding extra fields, changing the colours of the display and choosing report styles. Select the option to include sample data. This will allow you to explore the finished database. Take your time and read the advice that Access provides with each display. If you are in doubt, simply choose the Access default option.

3 When your switchboard appears explore the database you have created. Figure 57 shows you an input form for the Address Book database.

4 Try to:

■ input information (use the names and addresses you used to create a table if you have selected an address book)
■ preview the reports (Figure 56)

5 Identify the things that you would like to change and try to create a new, revised, database using the Wizard. See how much freedom the Wizard gives you.

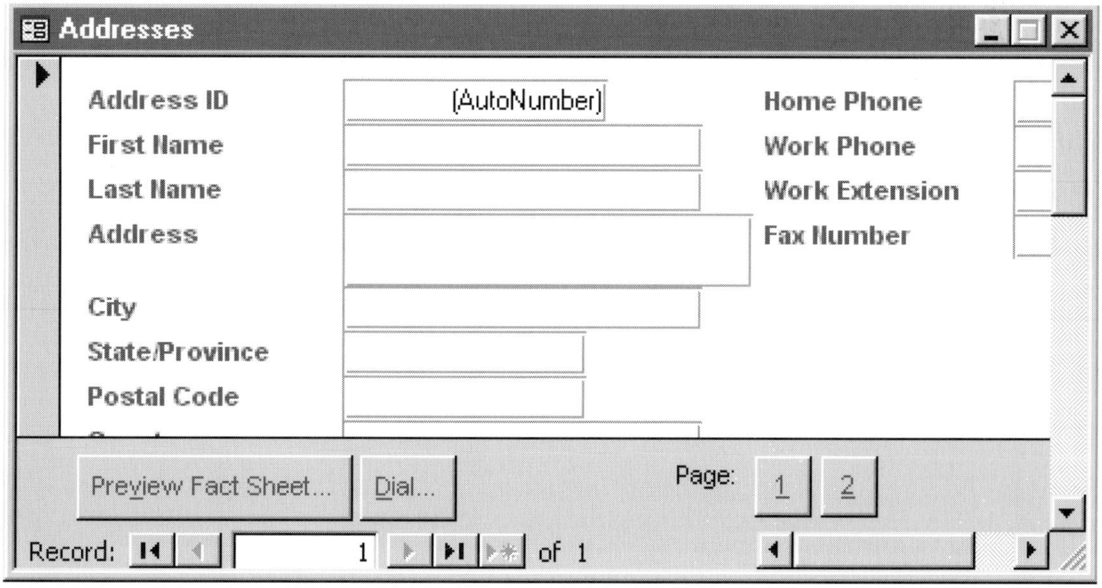

FIGURE 57 *Address book input form*

What next?

Now that you have some understanding of databases, try to identify databases when you come across them (e.g. contacting your telephone bank, completing forms which are designed to help database operators to input your details). Using **Database Wizard**, develop a database for your own use. Work with it over a period and decide if it is useful (e.g. compare a database of addresses with a conventional address book. Does it have advantages?).

SELF TEST QUESTIONS

If you want to test your understanding of this chapter try to answer these questions. The answers are given at the end of the book.

1   What is the main object of an Access database?

2   What are records divided into?

3   What is a Wizard?

4   What does a datasheet look like?

5   What is a relational database?

6   Describe a field.

7   What is a record?

8   How can tables be related to each other?

9   What types of data can you store in an Access database?

10 List the main methods of questioning the information stored in a database.

Painting and drawing

5

By the end of this chapter you should be able to:

- Load Paint

- Understand the main features of Paint

- Select the different drawing tools

- Change the drawing tool options including selecting different colours

- Use the drawing tools to produce a graphic image

- Describe clip art

- Capture screens using Print Screen

- Edit an image

We live in a visual world in which pictures are used extensively to convey information. Newspapers, magazines, newsletters and books all employ pictures to motivate readers and enhance communication. By using special applications, computers allow you to produce pictures, which are referred to as **graphics**, even if you have only modest artistic talent. These are called **design applications** and many different products are available. Windows 95 has a design application built into it called Paint (Figure 58).

Design applications provide you with tools to draw curves, circles, straight lines and rectangles with the minimum of skill. Equally importantly you can blow an image up on the screen so that you can touch up the tiny details and improve a picture significantly.

Design applications are available for many special and general purposes such as:

- creating your own greetings cards
- manipulating photographs

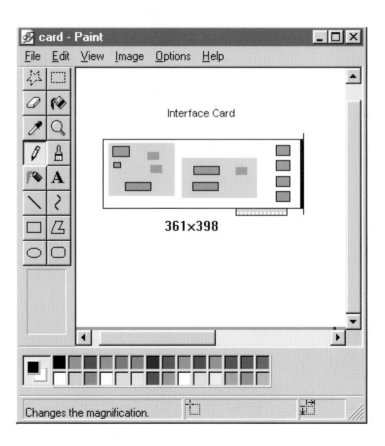

FIGURE 58 *Windows 95 Paint*

- designing your garden
- architectural design
- producing engineering drawings
- painting
- animating images.

The most advanced applications allow you to create three-dimensional images and to animate them. In movies this is often used to produce lifelike images but most packages cannot produce this type of quality. Many painting applications also allow you to **import** images from a scanner or a digital camera.

This chapter is divided into three tutorials, which include exercises that will allow you to practise many of the ideas presented in the text.

Tutorial 13 → Starting Paint

What is Paint?

Figure 59 shows the main features of Windows 95 Paint. This program comes as one of the accessories of the Windows 95 operating system. Paint can help you to create pictures, which you can copy and paste into many other Windows 95 applications such as Word.

The Paint program consists of six areas:

1 The **title bar**, which shows the name of the image. If you have not selected a name the image is called Untitled. You can give your image a name when you save it.

2 The **menu bar**, which is similar to that in other Windows applications and gives you control over the picture created.

3 The **drawing tool** area (Figure 60). The drawing tools allow you to create or import and modify images.

4 The **drawing area**. This is where you create or modify the images.

5 The **palette** (Figure 61). This is a paint box of different colours from which you choose the colours of your image.

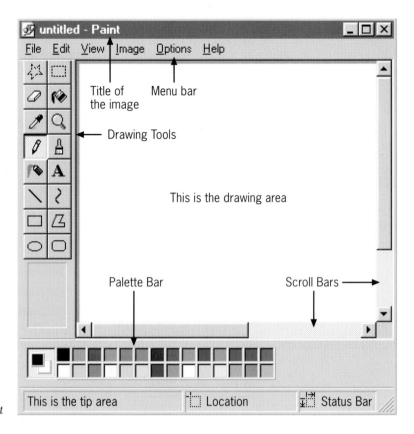

FIGURE 59 *Windows 95 Paint*

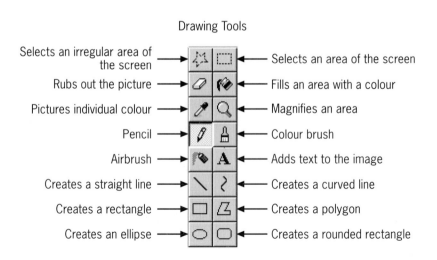

FIGURE 60 *The drawing tool area in Paint*

Colour Palette

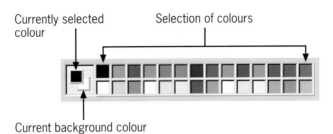

Currently selected colour

Selection of colours

Current background colour

FIGURE 61 *The palette area in Paint*

6 The **status line**. This gives you information about the tools you are using. In the left-hand box you are informed about the drawing tool and in the right-hand box about the position of the drawing.

EXERCISE 27

Explore Windows 95 Paint

■ Duration: 60

1 If you click on the **Start** button and then select **Programs**, a list of programs will appear to the right. Move your mouse pointer up the list until you locate **Accessories**. When your pointer is resting on **Accessories** another list will appear to the right. Move the pointer until it rests on **Paint** then click. Windows 95 Paint will appear (Figure 59).

2 Paint will either fill the whole screen or appear within a window. If the latter happens, click on the maximise button in the top right-hand corner of the window to expand the image so that it fills the whole screen.

3 Explore the menu items by clicking on each. **File** and **Edit** are similar to those in other applications, but **View**, **Image** and **Options** are different.

4 Click on each tool (Figure 59) and see how it is described in the Status line box which gives hints and tips at the bottom of the screen. For example:

 Changes to magnification

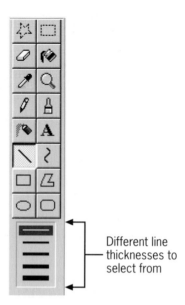

Different line
thicknesses to
select from

FIGURE 62 *Extra features on the Paint drawing toolbar*

5 If you click on some of the drawing tools you will see that the area below the tool box changes. For example, clicking on the straight line tool provides you with a series of different thicknesses of line to select from (Figure 62).

6 Other tools offer different choices:

- rubber – erasers in a range of sizes
- magnifier – different degrees of magnification
- brush – different sizes and shapes of paint brush
- airbrush – different paint patterns
- curved and straight lines – different thicknesses of line
- rectangle, polygon, ellipse and rounded corner rectangle – empty, filled or filled without an outline.

7 Try out the various tools – it does not matter if you make a mess.

8 Continue until you have tried all the tools.

Tutorial 14 → Using Paint

How do you get started?

When you first load Paint the working area is blank and the top line tells you your picture is called Untitled (see Figure 59). Paint starts with the pencil drawing tool ready to use; if you move your mouse the pencil moves around the drawing area. If you want to draw you must hold down the left mouse button and move the mouse. The cursor will leave behind it a line, in the same way that moving a pencil over a piece of paper produces a line. If you want to stop, release the button – you can then move the mouse without drawing lines.

Change the drawing tool by clicking on any of the drawing tool icons (see Figure 62). All of them work in the same way that the pencil tool does: that is, you move them using the mouse. Activate each tool by holding down the left mouse button and stop by releasing the button.

Some of the tools provide you with different options which appear at the bottom of the drawing tool area. If you click on the line drawing tool, a series of options become available, such as different thicknesses of line (shown in Figure 62). These allow you to choose which thickness of line to draw by clicking on the option. You can use a mixture of different line thicknesses – or any other options – by releasing the left button (i.e. stop drawing), then clicking on a new option and continuing your drawing. Figure 63 shows a drawing using different line thicknesses.

You can also draw in a range of colours. Again, it is simply a matter of clicking on the colour of your choice in the colour palette (Figure 61). You can combine colour, drawing tool and drawing option within a single image simply by clicking on the options in any combination.

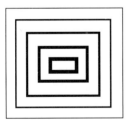

FIGURE 63 *A drawing prepared with all five line thicknesses available in Paint*

EXERCISE 28

Drawing

■ Duration 30 minutes

1   Try to draw the images shown in Figures 64, 65 and 66.

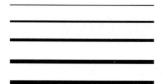

FIGURE 64 *This figure requires you to use the line tool and all five options*

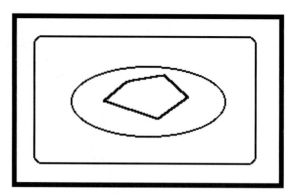

FIGURE 65 *To draw this figure you must use the rectangle, ellipse, polygon and rounded rectangle tools with some of options from the line tool. Experiment with the four tools until you are confident you can use them*

What is clip art?

FIGURE 66 *To produce this figure you need to use the ellipse, curved line and colour fill, in combination with a colour from the palette*

An alternative to drawing your own images is to use **clip art**. This is a package of standard images which you can buy or which is often given away free with computer magazines. Thousands of clip art images can be bought on a CD-ROM. You can load clip art images into applications such as Word and Paint. If you load an image into Paint you can change it, so it is possible for someone with very little artistic skill to produce high-quality images using clip art.

In order to load clip art from a CD-ROM click on **Open** and select the CD-ROM drive, which is often **D:**. You can then select from the images stored on the disk. Once you have a loaded an image, you will find the magnifier is a very useful tool as it allows you to focus on a small area of the image (Figure 67). As computer images are made of many dots (called **pixels**) which are rectangular in shape (Figure 68),

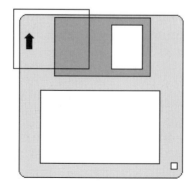

FIGURE 67 *Images are made up of individual pixels*

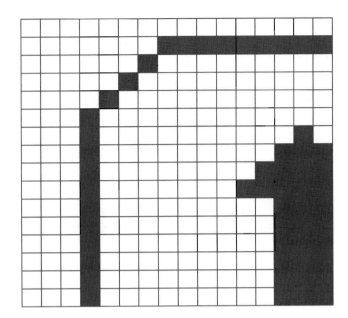

FIGURE 68 *A drawing of a floppy disk prepared using Paint showing individual pixels*

you can edit the picture dot by dot. This is similar to painting by numbers or colouring in book pictures. It is a slow process but one which allows you to produce good-quality images. Figure 68 shows an image of a floppy disk which was produced by drawing a rectangle and editing the individual pixels to produce a fairly reasonable image.

Another approach to creating pictures is to use **screen captures**. These are images produced by taking a type of photograph of the computer screen. You can take a screen capture using specialist software or by using Print Screen, which you will find on the top line of keys to the right-hand side of the keyboard.

How do you capture a screen?

If you press the print screen key once, you take a photographic image of the screen you are currently watching. To view the image you need to use the clipboard viewer. This is located in the Accessories menu within the Paint program. When you capture a screen, it is stored on the **clipboard**, which is a special area of Windows. Every time you use copy or cut in any Windows application your selection is stored on the clipboard. If you click once on **Clipboard Viewer** you will see that it opens up in the same way as other Windows applications and shows you what you have captured. It may open in a window (which you can maximise) or it may fill the whole screen. The clipboard can store only one image at a time – however, you can save the images by clicking on **File** and then **Save As** within Clipboard Viewer. The screen capture is saved in a file with the extension of .clp (i.e. clipboard) and can be loaded only into Clipboard Viewer.

Graphic images are all saved as files. However, there are a number of different types (**formats**) of file. The format is shown by the final three letters which are known as an **extension**. Paint is only able to load images stored with the extension .bmp or Windows bitmap. Word can import a wider range of image format, including:

- Windows bitmaps files with extension – .bmp
- tag image file format – .tif
- PC Paintbrush files – .pcx
- Corel Draw files – .cdr
- Windows metafiles – .wmf.

To make more use of screen captures taken with Print Screen you need to paste them into other applications. You can paste screen captures into Paint, so if you load Paint and click on **Edit** and then **Paste** the image captured will appear in the drawing area. However, because the clipboard can hold only one image at a time you need to be careful you have captured the image you want. Once you have pasted the image into Paint you can edit the picture.

EXERCISE 29

Capturing and editing pictures

■ Duration: 45 minutes

1 Choose a screen and, using Print Screen, capture it.

2 Load Clipboard Viewer and see if you have successfully captured your chosen screen. If you have not been successful, try again.

3 Exit Clipboard Viewer by clicking on **File** and then **Exit**.

4 Load Paint and paste the captured image into the drawing area. You may be asked this question:

The image in the clipboard is larger than the bitmap. Would you like the bitmap enlarged?

If you are asked this question click on **Yes**; your image will appear. It will be larger than the drawing area so you will need to use the scroll bars (both horizontal and vertical) to see all of it.

5 Edit some part of the image (e.g. use the eraser). For example, if you have captured from a Windows application remove some of the menu items.

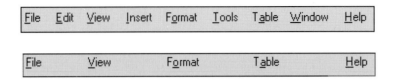

6 Try to edit the image so you cannot tell that something has been removed. You will need to use the magnifier, eraser and colour fill, and perhaps some other tools. Experiment and see what you can achieve.

| Tutorial 15 → | Advanced features |

What are the advanced features of Paint?

Although Paint is a basic drawing application you have a number of powerful features at your fingertips. The main features are:

- copy and paste
- cut and paste
- copying and cutting irregular chunks
- saving part of an image
- creating new colours
- painting images.

The two main tools you will use are the irregular and rectangular selection tools. Both allow you to choose an area of an image that you can then copy or cut and paste into another part of the picture or into a new image.

Once you have selected an area with either of these tools you can choose to save it as a separate image rather than cut or copy it. You do this by clicking on **Edit** and then **Copy to**. You will be asked to give the new image a file name.

EXERCISE 30

Copying, cutting and pasting

■ Duration: 45

1 Draw the image below.

2 Now copy the image by using the rectangular selection tool. You do this by clicking on the tool. A new mouse pointer will appear: it is shaped rather like gunsights. Position the pointer at one corner of the image and, holding down the left mouse button, move it to the diagonally opposite corner and release your finger. The image is now surrounded by a rectangle. You will find that you can drag the rectangle around the drawing area by placing the pointer inside it. The pointer will change shape again, and if you hold down the left mouse button you can move the image to any part of the area you wish. Try moving it around the area until you are confident.

3 Repeat this operation using the irregular selection tool. Activate the tool by clicking on the icon – the mouse pointer again changes to resemble a gunsight. If you hold down the left mouse button you can draw around any area you want to cut or copy. Once you have encircled an area, release the button and a rectangle will appear enclosing your chosen area.

4 Once you have enclosed your area in the rectangle click on **Edit**. You will find you have a choice of **Cut**, **Copy**, **Paste**, **Copy to** and **Paste From**. **Cut**, **Copy** and **Paste** work in the same way as they do in Microsoft Word and Excel. **Copy to** and **Paste From** are additional functions. **Copy to** allows you to save part of an image captured by cut or copy to a new file. **Paste From** allows you to paste an image saved to a file into your picture.

5 When you paste an image from **Cut**, **Copy** or **Paste From** it appears inside a rectangle and you need to drag it to the position you chose.

6 Experiment with these tools to produce the image below.

7 Continue to experiment until you are confident that you can select, cut, copy, paste and drag images or parts of images around the area.

How do you change colours?

If you are not happy with the selection of colours in the palette you can mix your own by clicking on **Options** and then **Edit Colors** when the screen shown in Figure 69 appears.

The top part of the display shows you the basic colours available. If you want to produce your own shades then click on **Define Custom Colors >>**. A new area opens up to the right of the display (Figure 70). This is like mixing paints to make a new shade. Your first step is to set the degree of brightness of the colour – simply click within the rectangular bar on the right edge of the display. This shows you brightness, from black at the bottom to white at the top. Choose the degree of brightness you want. Now move your mouse into the multicoloured rectangle and move it around, watching the small square below – this shows the colour you are producing. Once you have mixed the colour you want, add it to your palette by clicking on the **Add to Custom Colors** button. You can mix up to 14 new colours. When you return to the main display you will see that the new colours have been added to the palette.

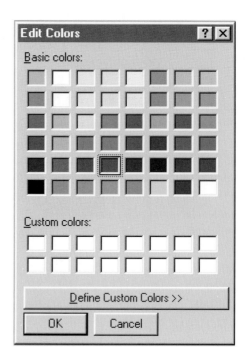

FIGURE 69 *Editing colours in Paint*

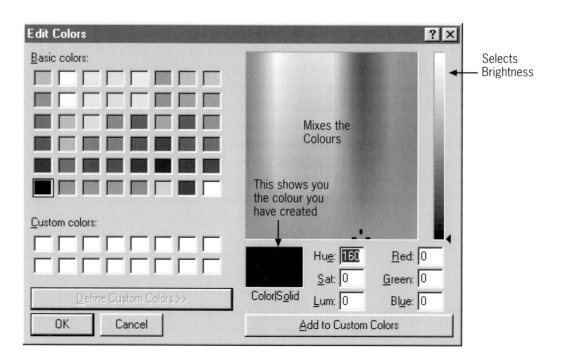

FIGURE 70 *Producing your own colours in Paint*

EXERCISE 31

Mixing colours

■ Duration: 30

1 Try to produce four new colours based on red, black, blue and yellow.

2 Experiment until you have shades that you like and then use them to paint with using the Painting tools (e.g. brush and fill tools).

What next?

This chapter has introduced you to Paint, which is an unsophisticated drawing application. There are many others which offer far more. However, if you are like me and only want to use clip art or add the occasional illustration to some writing, then Paint provides all the features you need.

SELF TEST QUESTIONS

If you want to test your understanding of this chapter try to answer these questions. The answers are given at the end of the book.

1 What is clip art?

2 How can Paint contribute to other Windows applications?

3 Name three tools that Paint provides to help you create or edit images.

4 What are the individual dots that make up an image called?

SELF TEST QUESTIONS – continued

5 List the options available with the line drawing tool.

6 Which application would you use to view screen captures stored on the clipboard?

7 Where are colours stored in Paint?

8 What shapes can the two selection tools enclose in order to copy part of an image?

9 How do you produce new colours in Paint?

10 Here is a list of graphics formats:

- Windows bitmaps files with extension – .bmp
- tag image file format – .tif
- PC Paintbrush files – .pcx
- Corel Draw files – .cdr.
- Windows metafiles – wmf.

Which of these graphics formats does Paint use?

The Internet

By the end of this chapter you should be able to:

- Understand the nature of the Internet

- Access the World Wide Web through a browser

- Effectively search the World Wide Web

- Navigate around a web site

- Download chosen information from the Internet

The Internet is a world-wide communication network which links together many millions of individuals and organisations. It is growing rapidly, with many thousands of people gaining access to the network every day. It came into existence as part of a research project to link together universities and other research groups. From this beginning the Internet has expanded to circle the globe and to connect almost every possible type of organisation and individual.

The Internet allows you to share information, send messages, hold discussions, buy goods and services, learn new subjects and socialise. All this is possible from your own home with the right equipment. Anyone can learn how to use the Internet. It's considerably less difficult than driving a car!

The chapter is divided into three tutorials, which include exercises that will allow you to practise many of the ideas presented in the text. Each exercise indicates how long it should take you to complete. Exercises can be undertaken anywhere you can gain access to the Internet – work, college, library, cybercafe or home. At the end of the chapter is a series of short questions to check your knowledge.

Tutorial 16 → What is the Internet

The Internet is a means of linking a large number of computers and computer networks so that from your own machine you can access information stored on these computers. It is essentially a control mechanism that allows you to view and transfer information. The Internet consists of a number of services and parts. The main elements are:

- electronic mail (**e-mail**), which allows you send and receive messages
- telnet, which lets you remotely use another computer attached to the Internet as if you were there
- file transfer protocol (FTP), with which you can move files of information between computers attached to the Internet
- mail groups, news groups (often called Usenet) and chat, parts of the Internet that permit you to communicate with people having similar interests
- the World Wide Web (WWW, or 'the Web'), which incorporates all of the above.

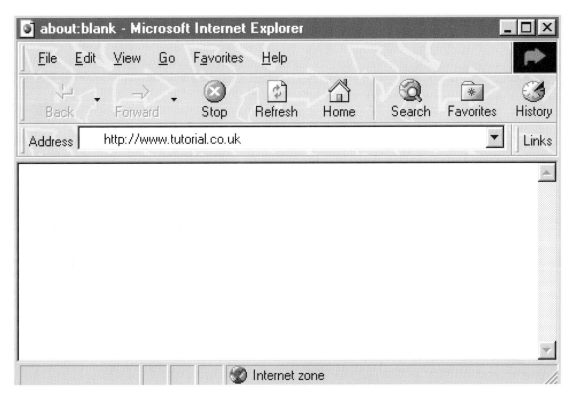

FIGURE 71 *Microsoft Internet Explorer*

The WWW consists of millions of sites. Each site comprises groups of documents designed using a specialist programming language called **hypertext markup language** (or HTML). The sites can be viewed using a **browser**, which is a program designed to allow you to access WWW documents anywhere in the world. The two most popular browsers are:

- Microsoft Internet Explorer (Figure 71)
- Netscape Navigator (Figure 72).

Web sites are often based on large powerful computers operated by major companies, universities, governments and international organisations. However, many individuals run web sites using their own home computers and many Internet providers offer space for individual and small company sites on their equipment.

For many people, the Web *is* the Internet in that it represents most of the areas that they will use. More correctly, the Internet is essentially the structure of computers and links while the Web is the contents.

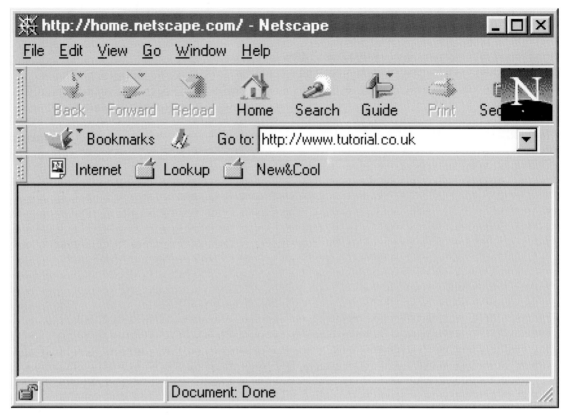

FIGURE 72 *Netscape Navigator*

What does the Internet offer you?

The Internet offers an exciting range of facilities for the user. The main features are:

- news – the latest world-wide news is available 24 hours a day, 7 days a week
- sport – everything from when tickets are on sale for the next international game to ball-by-ball commentary
- software – many software companies offer free upgrades of their products for existing customers as well as free demonstrations of their products to visitors to their sites
- education – interactive education is rapidly developing
- shopping – you can already buy a huge selection of books, music and computer equipment on the Web. Other products are becoming available every day
- information – almost every conceivable subject can be

found on the Internet; it is like owning an enormous
library
- ■ hobbies – most interests and hobbies have Web sites
waiting for you to use
- ■ communication – fast, reliable and cheap communication
to link you to people with similar interests.

The negative aspects are that the Internet also contains
offensive material in the form of pornography and offensive
political views. If you are going to give your children access
you may need to supervise their use or be prepared for them
to occasionally come across some unpleasant material.

What do you need to connect to the Internet?

In order to connect yourself to the Internet you need a
personal computer such as a PC or an Apple Macintosh, a device
called a **modem**, a browser and some suitable communication
software. The communication software allows you send and
receive information and messages through an organisation
called an **internet service provider** (ISP). Modern computers
are often supplied with suitable communication and browser
software already installed (e.g. Windows 95). Many
educational organisations offer their students and staff access
to the Internet for free as part of their course of study or
employment. In a similar way many employees gain access to
the Internet through their work. There are many
commercial ISPs who offer access to the Internet from home
or elsewhere for a fee and even a few for free.

Computers designed to use Windows 95, Windows 98,
Windows NT or the Apple Macintosh operating systems have
the advantage of being designed to make them easy to link
with the Internet. However, you do not need the latest
computer to connect to the Internet. Many older computers
can make the connection, so don't rush out and buy a new
machine until you know you have to.

The key piece of equipment is the modem. It fits inside the
computer or comes as a small external box which is linked to
the computer by a cable. A modem normally connects your
computer to the Internet through the telephone system,
although it is sometimes used to link the computer through a
cable or digital channel. A modem converts your message into
a form which can be sent down the telephone line to the ISP's

modem, which converts it into a form which the ISP computer can understand. Modems are usually described in terms of their speed, bits per second (bps). Eight bits are needed to transfer one alphabetical character. A speed of 14,400 bits per second (14.4 kbps) will thus transfer approximately one A4 sheet of text per second. When you are communicating you have to wait for messages to be sent both ways, so the quality of the process depends on the speed; the faster the modem, the better. Most modems operate at 14,400bps, 28,800bps, 33,600bps or 56,000 bps.

The initial steps to accessing the Internet from Windows 95 depend on a number of variables – such as how the ISP's communication software has been installed, whether you are communicating from your workplace or a college and if you are using Windows Dial-up networking or bypassing it. This chapter assumes that you know how to make the connection. To access the system it frequently requires only clicking on an icon on the desktop or selecting Start and Programs.

What are ISPs?

ISPs are commercial companies who provide connections to the Internet for both individuals and companies. Charges and services vary between companies – in the UK there are several hundred ISPs to choose from. The typical choice is between paying a fee for unlimited access, paying by the hour or a combination of both. The ISP charge does not cover your telephone calls, although in the vast majority of cases the ISP will offer a way of accessing the Internet at local call rates. Many ISPs may offer you free space on their computers to establish your own web site. However, you need to develop the contents and structure of the site yourself.

The range of services offered by ISPs varies, with the larger providers offering access to all the Internet functions while some small providers only offer simple access to the Internet. When you are selecting an ISP you need to check what they provide and at what charge. A checklist of issues is given below:

1 Charges:

   ■ by the hour

   ■ unlimited access

- ▨ a combination

2 How to pay:

- ▨ annual fee

- ▨ monthly

- ▨ direct debit

- ▨ credit card

- ▨ cheque/cash

3 Cancellation period:

- ▨ frequently a notice period must be given

4 Installation:

- ▨ do they provide an easy-to-install system (i.e. a CD-ROM which only requires you to follow instructions displayed on the screen)?

5 Software: do they provide

- ▨ browser?

- ▨ e-mail?

- ▨ off-line editor?

- ▨ web editors for creating sites?

- ▨ access to mailgroups, newsgroups and chat?

6 E-mail:

- ▨ do you have to pay extra for e-mail?

- ▨ how many e-mail accounts are included (e.g. enough for the whole family)?

7 Telephone charges:

- ▨ are all charges at local call rates?

8 Free Web space to create your own site:

- ▨ how much space?

- ▨ personalised site names?

- ▨ are there any conditions?

9 Support services:

- very important that you have help available

- help line opening hours

10 Free magazines and software upgrades

The ISP provides you with the telephone number you use to connect to the Internet through its computer, the modem settings for your equipment plus a username and password. The password and username allow the ISP to identify that you are a subscriber and to give you access to their services.

There are also organisations called online service providers (OSPs) who provide access to the Internet for a fee (an example is America Online: AOL). These offer the same basic features of a connection to the Internet – e-mail and newsgroups. However, you often receive extra services (e.g. 24-hour news service) in addition to the basic services. OSPs tend to be large organisations operating across national boundaries while ISPs are usually national and sometimes cover only a small geographical area.

How do ISPs link you to the Internet?

ISPs provide you with a telephone number, which is called a point of presence (PoP). Your communication software dials this number when you try to access the Internet and links you through your modem to the ISP's computer. The ISP is linked to the Internet so you can make the next step to enter the Internet (Figure 73). Many ISPs have several PoPs throughout the country.

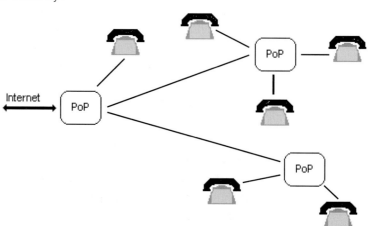

FIGURE 73 *Point of presence (PoP) links*

EXERCISE 32

Comparing Internet service providers

■ Duration: 30 minutes

1 Most libraries have copies of a range of computer magazines. Review the advertisements for ISPs.

2 Using the checklist on pages 112 to 114, draw up a table to compare the different facilities offered.

3 You might like to note down what information the advertisements do *not* provide about the service.

4 If you are seeking an ISP use steps 1–3 as the first part of the exercise and contact the most promising candidates to ask for more information.

5 Once further details have arrived use your table to complete your assessment.

What is a browser?

All browsers allow you to perform essentially the same tasks. Their fundamental role is to allow you to access a WWW site. Each site has a unique **address**, called a uniform resource locator (**URL**), which, when entered into the browser, allows it to find the site and view its contents.

If you look at Figures 71 and 72 you will notice boxes called **Address** and **Go To** respectively. This is where you enter the address of the web site you wish to access. In both examples you will see the address given as **http://www.tutorial.co.uk**. This shows you are seeking a WWW site called 'tutorial'. This is the **domain name**. The **co.uk** indicates that the site is a company in the UK. If you enter this address you will be taken to the **home page** of this site.

A home page can be considered as the contents page of the site in that it links you to the other parts of the site. If you extend the address (e.g. by typing **http://www.tutorial.co.uk/documents/example.html**) you can bypass the home page. This new address will take you deeper into the site to view a document called 'example'. All pages are viewed through the browser, which provides you with a number of tools to navigate the page. These are important in that a WWW site will often consist of many different pages linked together. Navigation devices are also built into the pages as links. The designer of a WWW site can create links from almost anything displayed on the page to any other part of the site – or of other sites. Links can also be made to other electronic information such as a picture or video. Many web pages use **frames**, whereby the page is divided into separate areas. Each area can act independently of the others. Often each area is surrounded by a border, which makes it easy to recognise, although this is not always the case.

Once you have selected a web site and entered the address (URL), the browser shows you what is happening by sending you messages on the bottom of the browser window. Internet Explorer 4.0 presents you with three messages to keep you informed in the bottom left hand corner of the window:

1 **Connecting to site** {number of site}   initial message

2 **Opening page http://**........................   after the system has located the site and page is being loaded

3 **Done** after page has been loaded.

While the page is being loaded, parts of the display begin to appear on the screen and slowly the whole page is revealed. The whole process can be very rapid (a few seconds) but if the page contains illustrations (graphics) it can take a while to fully load (over a minute), so be patient. To help you see the progress the system is making in loading a page, a blue bar slowly develops on the bottom of the browser window. This indicates the speed of loading.

The speed of loading a web page depends on several variables:

1 The speed of your modem

2 The nature of the web page (a text-only page will load faster than a page containing graphic pictures)

3 How many other people are accessing the same site at the same time

4 How many people are connected to the Internet

5 The capacity of your connection (telephone lines are the slowest).

It is possible to set your browser so that it loads only text from web sites (Table 1). This will considerably speed up loading.

Microsoft Internet Explorer 4.0	Netscape Navigator 4.0
1. View menu	1. File menu
2. Select Options	2. Preferences
3. Click on Advanced tab	3. Advanced option
4. In multimedia section, clear the checkboxes for Show Pictures	4. Clear checkbox – Automatically Load Images
5. Click on OK	5. Click on OK

However, pictures will be represented by small icons and will not contribute to your understanding of the information offered by the web site.

As the Internet began in the USA, more people use the Internet there than anywhere else so one tip to speed up your use of the Internet is to go on-line when there are fewer American users. If you remember the time differences between the UK and the USA you can work out when parts of the USA are asleep and not likely to be on line. The number of users in the UK peaks once children come home from school, so late afternoon and early evening are not good times for access. The morning is generally regarded as a reasonable time to go on line.

Figure 74 shows part of the 10 Downing Street web site. You will see that a number of words are underlined – this indicates that if you click on them you will jump to another part of the site or even to another site. The words usually change colour to indicate you have used that link. You normally make many jumps during a visit to a site. These are called **hypertext links**. There are two functions that you can see on the top of the browser (Figures 71 and 72) – **Forward** and **Back**. These allow you to move backwards or forwards around a web site one jump at a time. This is very useful if you get lost in a complex site. They also allow you to retrace your route from site to site.

How do you return to a useful web site?

Once you have located a useful site the browser provides you with a means of recording the address (URL) so that you can return to that site later. This is done in Microsoft Internet Explorer by clicking on the **Favorites** menu or button or the **Bookmark** menu in Netscape Navigator while on the site. Figure 75 shows the open **Favorites** menu. By clicking on **Add**

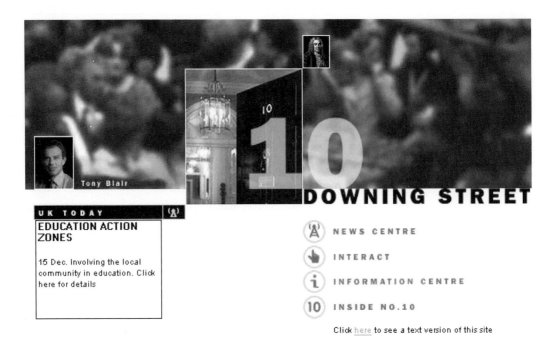

FIGURE 74 *Links on the 10 Downing Street home page*

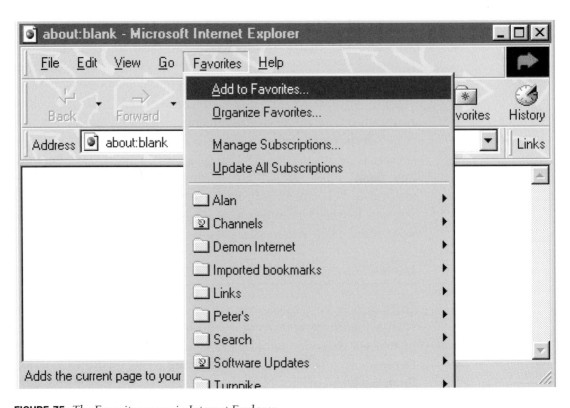

FIGURE 75 *The Favorites menu in Internet Explorer*

to Favorites you can record the site's address and the function will provide you with the means of organising your selected sites into folders using the **Organize Favorites** function. This is important, since with millions of sites to choose from it will not be long before you will have scores (if not hundreds) of chosen sites. When you want to return to a selected site, simply click on your choice in the Favorite or Bookmarked lists and the browser will find the site for you. You will see the chosen URL appear on the address line.

Both Netscape Navigator and Microsoft Internet Explorer keep a record (in history files) of the sites you have visited. This allows you to locate a site you have previously looked at but not made a Favourite or Bookmark. Both browsers provide several ways of accessing history lists.

■ ACCESSING HISTORY LISTS IN NETSCAPE NAVIGATOR 4.0

1 From address line, click on the down arrow (▼). A list of web sites you have previously visited will be revealed. This list shows only the main sites you have visited, whereas the other options provide the full list.

2 Click once on the right-hand mouse button (this is known as **right clicking**) on either the **Forward** or **Back** buttons. A full list of sites will appear.

■ ACCESSING HISTORY LISTS IN MICROSOFT INTERNET EXPLORER 4.0

1 Go from the address line in the same way as described for Netscape Navigator.

2 Right click on either the **Forward** or **Back** buttons. If you click on your chosen address in the list you will return to this site.

■ ERROR MESSAGES

The Web is in a constant state of change so it is not unusual to receive an error message saying that you cannot access the site. Error messages you might see include:

■ 'Not Found. The requested object does not exist on this server. The link you followed is either outdated, inaccurate, or the server has been instructed not to let you have it. Please inform the site administrator of the referring page.'

■ 'ERROR: The requested URL could not be retrieved.'

■ 'File Not Found. The requested URL example/file.html was not found on this server.'

The message that appears on the screen often gives you a clue as to what is wrong, but don't be surprised if it is meaningless. Error messages are often difficult to understand. Occasionally you will be able to access a site to find a message that tells you that it is under construction or that it has been moved. In this case the new address is usually given. However, no matter what happens just be relaxed and try another address or search the Web again to find the site you desire.

EXERCISE 33

Discover your browser

■ Duration: 30 minutes to 1 hour

1 Open your browser by clicking on the icon on the desktop. *Do not* log on to the Internet.

2 Start exploring the different features we have been discussing.
   a Click on each item of the menu on the bar at the top of the browser (**File Edit View Go Favorites Help**) and observe what is available.
   b Click on each button and see what happens. Try clicking on the **Channel** button in Microsoft Internet Explorer and observe what happens.

Explore the browser systematically so that you become familiar with what is available. Make notes if you find that useful.

If you place your mouse pointer over items, sometimes messages will appear to tell you what that area of the screen does.

Because you are not connected to the Internet you may see error messages. Just ignore and clear them by clicking on **OK**.

Tutorial 17 → # Web sites

What is a web site?

A web site is a collection of pages which are written in a language called hypertext markup language (HTML). Each page is a separate document. The main page of a web site is called the home page and has similar functions to those of the contents page in a book. Pages are **linked** together through a number of hypertext connections. These are shown by underlined words, coloured words, icons and graphic pictures. A useful way of identifying links is to watch the mouse pointer change shape. When the mouse pointer moves over a link the arrow shape changes to a pointing hand. The designer of a web site is free to provide as many or as few links as he or she wants so each site will consist of many access routes (Figure 76).

Pages are frequently many times longer than a book page. At first you may find this confusing when you are reading them. Designers often link different parts of the same page so that you can quickly jump to the information you choose. However, you might not be able to tell immediately where you have jumped to (a new page or another part of the same page). Links can be made between sites so that you can jump from one to another. This is so easy that it is often difficult to know you have changed sites.

When you are viewing a web page through a browser you can see only part of each page at any one time. Figure 77

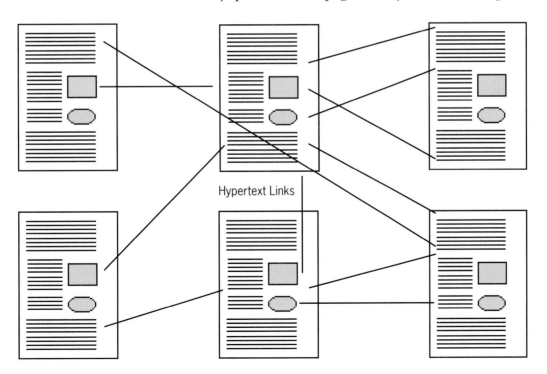

Hypertext Links

FIGURE 76 *Web page links*

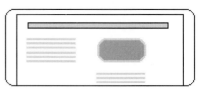

View of a Web Page through a browser at any moment

Full Web Page

FIGURE 77 *Only part of a web page is visible through a browser at any one time*

shows the view you have of a web page. You can view the whole page only by scrolling up or down the page or by using links to jump around the page. Each page is potentially a rich complex world and can be linked to many other pages and sites. This perhaps explains the excitement many users of the Internet find in visiting sites ('surfing the Web').

How do you download information?

There are several ways of recording information from a web site. These are:

- printing
- **downloading** the HTML file which forms the web page
- downloading other files attached to web sites.

▓ PRINTING

To print a page from a web site is straightforward. You need only click on the **Print** button or select the **Print** option within the **File** menu when you are accessing the page of your choice. If a printer is attached to your computer then it will print out the page. Since a web page can be any length the designer chooses, do not be surprised how many pages of print are produced from one web page – 20 or 30 A4 sheets is not unusual.

▓ DOWNLOADING FILES

If you would like to save an electronic copy of the page it is easy to do so. Click on the **Save as** option you will find under the **File** menu. It will save the page you are accessing as an

HTML file. To view the file, you need to use your browser but you do not have to access the Internet. Simply load the browser as a programme and enter the path and the name you have given the HTML file. The web page will be visible within your browser.

Designers often use web sites to distribute information and one way is to attach files to a page. If you want to download them you can usually do so by double-clicking on them and following the instructions which appear on the screen afterwards. Files are often in some type of word processor format or in the form of Adobe Acrobat files. Acrobat is a special program which allows you to create on-line documents. Acrobat files require a special reader to view them. However, readers are freely available on many web sites and often when designers provide Acrobat files to be downloaded they also offer access to the reader.

When you download files from the Web it is important to check that they are free from virus infection. In order to do this you must use your virus protection software. To download files without **virus protection** puts your system at risk. Viruses are normally associated with executable files (those ending in .exe) or macros of word processing and spreadsheet files (those ending in .doc, .dot and .xls).

Downloading normally means transferring a file from the Internet to your computer. When you want to transfer a file from your computer to a web site it is called **uploading**. In order to upload a file you need to use FTP. Most browsers have an FTP client which allows you to transfer a file to an FTP computer.

EXERCISE 34

Connecting to the World Wide Web

■ Duration: 2–3 hours

1 Choose one of the sites from the list of interesting World Wide Web Sites on page 132.

2 Enter the address in the browser and press Enter, double-click or click on **Open** (under the **File** menu).

3 Observe the process of accessing the site – make a note of what changes on the browser and how long the process takes.

4 Once your chosen site has been located then explore it by:
   a scrolling down the page

    b clicking on links (these are shown by underlined words, coloured words or pictures). You can do no harm by clicking on something which is not a link. Links are not always obvious.

5 Observe the site.
    a How long is a page?
    b What happens after you click on a link (watch the mouse pointer change shape when it is placed over a link)?
    c **Print** a web page
    d **Save** a web page as an HTML file.

6 Use the **Back** and **Forward** buttons to retrace your steps.

7 Mark the site as a favourite or a bookmark.

8 Leave the site and the WWW by choosing **File** and selecting the **Close** option. If you are connected from a college or your work then this is probably sufficient. If you are connected through your own ISP you will move back to its location and will need to repeat the process to leave the Internet. This process will depend on the ISP communication software (e.g. choose **File** and select **Exit** or **Close** or click on button marked **Disconnect**).

9 Practise accessing and exploring sites as much as you are able. There are few standards for site design and it is important to gain experience of all the different layouts and structures of sites.

10 Use the history function to see a list of your steps – access it using different methods and see if you can identify any differences in the different history lists.

Tutorial 18 → Searching and e-mail

What is a search engine?

The Web is a fascinating place where it is possible to find pages related to almost any topic. No matter what you are interested in (from postcard collecting to Scottish country

FIGURE 78 *AltaVista page*

dancing) there is someone out there who has created a site just for you. The difficulty is finding the site. You use a search engine to locate it.

A search engine is a method of searching the Web. It works on the basis of trying to match **keywords** that you enter with the contents of sites around the Web. Figure 78 shows you the AltaVista (http://altavista.digital.com) search engine. If you enter some keywords and click on **Search**, AltaVista will rapidly produce a list of sites which match the keywords (Figure 79). Often, the search will report matches with very large numbers of sites (as many as 1,000,000 hits – or more). The search engine will list them in the order it thinks are the closest matches. Most engines will allow you to search the initial list so that you can home in on the sites that contain your subject.

An example is trying to identify the Liverpool Football Supporters Club site using the Infoseek search engine (http://www.infoseek.com/):

1 Initial search on Infoseek
   ■ Keyword: football

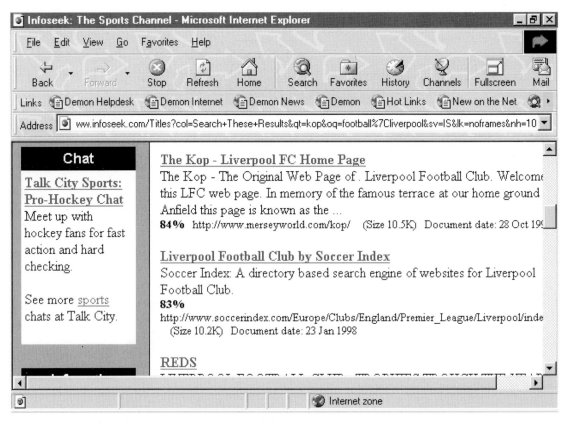

FIGURE 79 *Searching for Liverpool Supporters' Club sites*

■ Response: Infoseek found 824,473 web pages containing the word 'football'.

2 Refine the search by including only the web pages identified as containing the word 'football':

■ Search on Liverpool

■ Response: Infoseek found 473 football web pages containing the word 'Liverpool'.

3 Refine the search by including only the sites with words 'football' and 'Liverpool':

■ Search on Kop

■ Response: Infoseek found 39 football and Liverpool pages containing word 'Kop'.

Most search engines will offer you advice about how to conduct a search and how to interpret results. They provide a lot of specialist services to help you find what you want. Have a go and see what you can find.

There are many search engines. You need to explore them to identify those that meet your needs. Here are the URLs of a few:

- AltaVista – http://www.altavista.digital.com/
- Excite – http://www.excite.com/
- HotBot – http://www.hotbot.com/
- Infoseek – http://www.infoseek.com/
- Lycos – http://www-uk.lycos.com/
- Northern Lights – http://www.nlsearch.com/
- Webcrawler – http://www.webcrawler.com/

Search engines can also be used to find newsgroup messages and even individual e-mail addresses. There are several search engines which specialise in locating e-mail addresses. For example:

- Bigfoot – http://www.bigfoot.com/
- Four11 – http://www.Four11.com/
- Whowhere – http://www.whowhere.com/

Microsoft Internet Explorer 4.0 has a function called QuickSearch. If this button is clicked a list of search engines will appear (Figure 80). This provides a shortcut. If you type the shortcut (e.g. av for AltaVista) into the address box, leave a

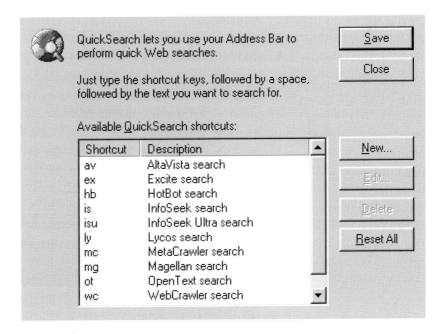

FIGURE 80 *Internet Explorer's QuickSearch*

space then enter your keywords and press return, a search engine will seek a match.

For example, keying **is Liverpool** will initiate a search for web pages containing the word 'Liverpool' using the Infoseek search engine.

You can also search for sites by using **Internet directories**. A directory is essentially a list of sites organised into categories. Search a directory by choosing a broad subject (such as computers) and you will be presented with a list of choices. By making successive choices you can arrive at the site you want. One of the best known directories is Yahoo (http://www.yahoo.com or http://www.yahoo.co.uk, which is the search engine for UK sites). Many search engines also provide directories.

EXERCISE 35

Searching the Internet

■ Duration: 2–3 hours

1 Pick a subject to find on the Web (e.g. a sport, fan club, music, tourist information).

2 Choose one of the search engines listed earlier and enter the address into your browser.

3 Once you access the search engine, explore the site and note what it offers you (e.g. news, other information and focusing your search).

4 Once you have explored the site enter your keywords (hint: pick the obvious and see what happens).

5 Observe the results of your search.
   a How many pages have been located?
   b How is the list of matches displayed?

6 See if you can refine your search:
   a by changing your keywords
   b by searching the matched pages with new keywords
   c by using the help/assistance offered by the search engine.

7 Choose another search engine and repeat the process. You can jump from one site directly to another by entering the new search engine's address in the normal way. Do this two or

three times, compare the results of the same searches using different engines and find out what each site offers you.

What is e-mail?

E-mail is a major part of the Internet; it provides you with a way of sending messages thousands of miles in minutes. It is essentially a world-wide electronic postal service which costs virtually nothing to use. Most ISPs provide you with an e-mail account as part of your fee for gaining access to the Internet. However, there is no guarantee that the recipient will read or answer your message. Chapter 7 covers the topic in more depth.

What other services does the Internet offer you?

■ NEWS AND MAIL GROUPS

You can join newsgroups and mailgroups, which are different ways for you to communicate to other Internet users who have similar interests. Newsgroups are like large noticeboards on which you can pin messages and read other people's messages any time you want. Mailgroups are also designed to allow you to talk to people with the same interests but they operate differently from newsgroups. In a mailgroup, you e-mail a message to a central address and everyone who enrols in the group receives the message.

There are tens of thousands of both types of group and some ISPs offer access to both newsgroups and mailgroups. Search engines often allow you to search for groups which interest you. DejaNews (http://www.dejanews.com/) allows you to search thousands of different newsgroups while lists of mailgroups are held on the Delphi site (http://www.delphi.com/navnet/faq/list.html).

■ USENET

Usenet is a world-wide network of newsgroups and contains thousands of newsgroups from which you can choose. Some ISPs offer access to Usenet so that as soon as you are on-line you can join newsgroups. There are groups for every conceivable hobby and interest. However, some groups may contain material that is inappropriate for children, so be careful if you are going to allow your children unsupervised access. To gain an overview about a newsgroup read the 'Frequently Asked

Questions' (FAQ) section or simply read the messages for a while. This is called 'lurking', but everyone does it.

■ CHAT

Chat is another way of communicating across the Internet. It normally takes the form of a live 'conversation', which is carried out by typing messages. In order to take part you need special software which you can often download free from Web sites. The chat programmes operate with your browser. If you are interested in getting started try visiting http://www.ichat.com/ or use a search engine to locate chat sites. A simple way of trying out chat is available through the Yahoo directory site (www.yahoo.com).

The original home of chat is Internet Relay Chat (IRC), which is a separate part of the Internet with its own computers and systems. At one time this was the only way of chatting on-line. However, chat is now available in the Web with many ISPs and especially OSPs providing their own chat areas as well as access to IRC.

■ SOUND AND VIDEO

You are not limited to typing messages to communicate with other Internet users. You can send sound and video over the Internet if you have the right equipment. For voice messages you need a fast PC with a **sound card** and microphone, a fast modem (at least 28,800 bps) and some telephone software.

At the moment the quality of both sound and video communications tends to be relatively poor, although it is improving rapidly. Installing the systems is not straightforward so it is normally not suitable for beginners.

How reliable is the information on the WWW?

Anyone can create a web site. There are no restrictions as to what you put on your site and nobody checks across the Web to ensure standards, although national governments are seeking to legislate to stop racist or other offensive material appearing. This freedom is a major strength of the Web, and yet it is also a significant weakness. The information available on the Web is only as accurate as the person who put it up. You should therefore be careful about how much reliance you place on what you read.

What next?

This chapter has introduced you to a range of key concepts. To increase your understanding and skill in using the Internet requires practice, so you should

- visit different web sites and observe their differences
- use the different search engines and compare their results
- try shopping on-line and contrast it with visiting a shop in person
- join a newsgroup or a mailgroup
- experience chat.

It is unlikely that all the elements of the Internet will be useful to you but experience them before you decide.

SELF TEST QUESTIONS

If you want to test your understanding of this chapter try to answer these questions. The answers are given at the end of the book.

1 List the main aspects of the Internet.

2 Name the two most popular Web browsers.

3 What does URL stand for?

4 What language is used to write web pages?

5 What is an ISP?

6 Give the name for the links between web pages.

7 When placed over a link, what shape does the pointer change into?

8 In your web browser, what is a 'favorite'?

9 What is the function of HotBot?

10 What is a mailgroup?

Some interesting World Wide Web sites

■ BOOKSHOPS

Amazon on-line bookshop   http://www.amazon.com/
Barnes and Noble bookshop   http://www.barnesandnoble.com/
Book Stacks Unlimited   http://www.books.com/

■ COMPUTERS

Computers on-line shops   http://www.compusa.com/
    http://www.cdw.com/

■ EDUCATION

The Times Educational Supplement   http://www.tes.co.uk

■ FREEBIES

A list of all freebies available on the Internet
http://home.netvigator.com/~artyeung/free/index.html

■ GOVERNMENT

Central Office of Information   http://www.coi.gov.uk
Downing Street   http://www.number-10.gov.uk
Government   http://www.open.gov.co.uk

■ GUIDES

Guide to the best sites on the Web   http:www.netguide.com/
100 best sites   http://www.web100.com/

■ LANGUAGES

English–Arabic bilingual journal   http://ozemail.co.au/~fouad/

■ MAGAZINES

Exchange and Mart
http://www.exchangeandmart.co.uk
New Scientist   http://www.newscientist.com
The Economist   http://www.economist.com

■ MUSIC

New Musical Express   http://www.nme.co.uk
Music stores on-line   http://www.cdnow.com/
    http://www.musicblvd.com/
    http://www.cdworld.com/
    http://www.emusic.com/
Internet music (links to lots of sites)
http://www.teleport.com/~celinec/music.shtml

■ NEWSPAPERS

The Daily Telegraph	http://www.telegraph.co.uk
The Guardian	http://www.guardian.co.uk
Sporting Life	http://www.sporting-life.com
The Star	http://megastar.co.uk
The Times	http://www.the-times.co.uk

■ SHOPPING

Virtual Shopping Emporium   http://www.virtualemporium.com/

■ SPORT

Fantasy Football   http://fantasyfootball.co.uk

List of Football Club sites

http://www.marwin.ch/sport/fb/teams.html#eng

■ TELEVISION

BBC On-line   http://www.bbc.co.uk

E-mail

By the end of this chapter
you should be able to:

■ Understand what e-mail is and what it requires

■ Send an e-mail

■ Read and reply to an e-mail

■ Attach a file to an e-mail

■ Add an address to the address book

■ Find an e-mail address using the Internet

Throughout this chapter we will be using mainly Microsoft systems and products as examples of how to use the Internet. However, the functions described are available on a number of other systems so if you are using other products, look for similar names, buttons or menus. Broadly similar features will be there although perhaps in slightly different places. Do not be put off – have a go.

E-mail is a major part of the Internet. It is essentially a world-wide electronic postal service which costs virtually nothing to use. Most Internet service providers (ISPs) provide you with an e-mail account as part of your fee for gaining access to the Internet and often you can have accounts for all members of your family and more. It is perfectly possible to have a personal account, a work account, a hobby account etc. However, this depends on your contract with the provider. Once you begin to use e-mail it will become obvious what advantages it has over the post, telephone and fax. E-mail is:

- almost free
- very fast; an e-mail can be delivered thousands of miles away in minutes
- not limited to text; pictures, sounds and video can be attached to an e-mail
- not restricted by time; you can send a message any time you like
- able to send one message to as many recipients as you want.

The growth in electronic commerce (**e-commerce**) indicates that use of e-mail, will continue to grow rapidly. It is already possible to buy books, music compact discs, holidays and even houses using e-mail, and applications are expanding with each passing day. Many new computer users find e-mail the most useful application that they initially encounter. The main negative development is that you do receive unsolicited e-mail advertisements (called **Spams**), which always seem to be about get rich quick schemes or sex. However, e-mail is far quicker to bin than paper junk mail!

This chapter is divided into three tutorials, which include exercises that will allow you to practise many of the ideas presented in the text.

Tutorial 19 → ## What is e-mail?

E-mail is very similar to surface mail in that in order to use it you must follow a standard agreed method. E-mail requires:

- an address
- an electronic post box and postal service which is provided by the ISP.

An e-mail address has a very specific structure:

name@organisation.type.country
Name	Organisation	Type	Country
example@	tutorial.	co.	uk

Here is a typical e-mail address:

alan@pace.isp.co.uk.

This tells you that my name is Alan, my account name is pace and my provider is isp, which is a company (co.) based in the United Kingdom (uk). Some providers do not offer you the opportunity to have your own account name – in that case the address would be alan@isp.co.uk.

If your e-mail is provided by your employer or educational institution then the address is shortened by replacing your account and ISP names with the organisation's title. E-mail addresses are similar to postal addresses in that they indicate who you are sending mail to and where they are. An e-mail address indicates through codes the type of organisation (for example, .org means charity or other non-profit organisation) and what country they are based in (for example, .be means Belgium). Other codes for organisations and countries are shown in Table 2.

It is very important to be accurate with e-mail addresses. You may be able to send a postal letter successfully with an incorrect address because the postman will recognise the mistake, but the electronic 'postman' can work only with correct addresses. If an e-mail is not delivered then you will probably get an error message. The main reason is an incorrect address but it is also sometimes due to problems with the recipient's computer.

To use e-mail you need special software. Both the main browsers (Netscape Navigator and Microsoft Internet Explorer

Mail

TABLE 2 *E-mail codes for organisations and countries*

Code	Organisation type	Code	Country
.ac	University/academic	.au	Australia
.com	American company	.cn	Canada
.edu	Educational institution	.dk	Denmark
.gov	Government	.fr	France
.mil	Military	.hk	Hong Kong
.net	Network	.jp	Japan
		.nz	New Zealand
		.uk	United Kingdom
			Most American addresses do not include a country code

– see Chapter 6) have e-mail facilities built into them. Internet Explorer is accompanied by an e-mail system called Outlook Express. This is accessed by clicking on the Mail icon or by clicking on **Start** and **Programs** and selecting Microsoft Outlook by double clicking. If you double-click on the **Mail** icon the e-mail system will appear (Figure 81).

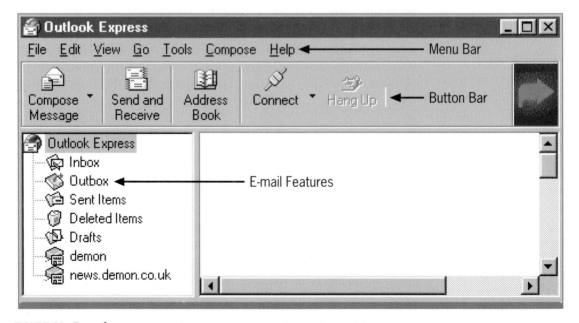

FIGURE 81 *E-mail system*

The basic structure of e-mail shown in Figure 81 is common to most systems. The key functions are similar to the process of sending normal surface post.

- Inbox: your letter box
- Outbox: mail tray in an office
- Compose: write your message
- Send: post your letter into postbox
- Receive: pick up your mail
- Address book: similar to a paper address book.

The system also keeps a record of what you have sent, and you can save mail you have received or delete it.

The etiquette of using e-mail ('netiquette') is different from that of surface mail, reflecting the changes between the two approaches. It is very easy to send an e-mail so that many people respond to any suggestion with vigour. Angry responses are called **flames** and the Internet can seem to be full of people who will send off a fierce response to even the mildest idea.

Good netiquette is based on:

- always being polite
- never sending unsolicited e-mails without at least apologising for them. You will soon discover that e-mail is very suitable for sending junk advertising mail
- not over-reacting to messages you receive.

EXERCISE 36

**Exploring
Outlook Express**

- Duration: 45 minutes

1 It is important to understand how your e-mail system is structured. You should spend some time exploring the structure of the various functions and what lies behind each menu choice and button.

2 The interface is divided into several areas:

- menu bar (which is similar to that of the other Windows applications you have studied)
- a series of large buttons (e.g. **Send** and **Receive**) immediately below the menu bar
- two windows – the left-hand one with a list of the major components of the system (the final items may be different in your system since they refer to the ISP); the right-hand window provides access to your messages.

3 Systematically click on each of the components in the bottom left-hand window (**Inbox, Outbox, Sent** items, etc) and observe what happens to the row of large buttons above the window. As you change items the buttons will sometimes grey out to indicate that they are not available.

4 The message window will probably remain blank if you have never sent a message. There may well be, however, messages sent by your ISP. Typically messages will be seen when you click on Inbox and will concern topics such as 'Welcome to Microsoft Outlook Express'.

5 Double-click on any message and observe what happens. You can close the message by closing the window, which will return you to the main Outlook Express display.

6 Explore the functions of the large buttons and menu bar and notice that they are largely duplicated. There is no right or wrong way of using them: *you* choose what is best for *you.*

7 Continue the investigation until you have an overview of the e-mail system.

Tutorial 20 → Sending and receiving e-mail

How to send an e-mail

The e-mail system provides a writing pad onto which you can write your message. In Outlook Express you click on Compose Message and a message pad opens up (Figure 82). This is divided into two main areas.

The top contains information on where you are sending the message – enter the person's e-mail address here (in the **To:** line in Figure 82). If you want to send a copy of your message to another person you enter their address in the **CC:** line. The main recipient is informed that the message has been copied to the other person. There is a special category called a blind copy (**BCC:** line) in which the main recipient is not informed that it has been copied. The last line on the top of

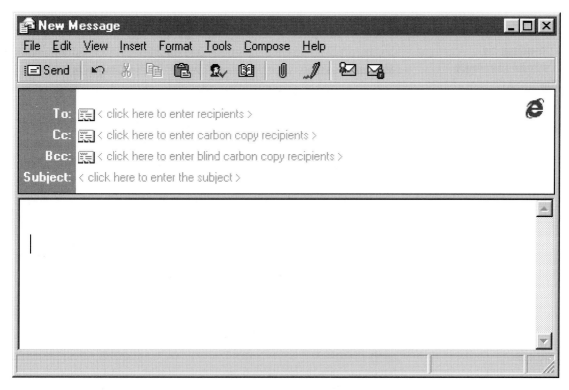

FIGURE 82 *Mail pad*

the pad is the subject of the message. You type the title of your message in here. This is important because people who use e-mail often receive scores of messages every day and these are presented to them as a list of titles. If you want your message read quickly then make your subject stand out (e.g. URGENT).

You write your message in the bottom half of the pad. There are no standards of layout for e-mail as there are for letters. However, remember to be clear and polite – it is easy to be more offensive and abrupt in e-mail than in most media. Once you have written your message you can send it immediately by clicking on the Send button.

You can either write messages on-line (i.e. connected to the Internet) and send them immediately across the network or you can work off-line. Off-line simply means you are preparing your messages in advance and as soon as you access the Internet they will be sent. The bonus is that you reduce your telephone call charges. However, you need to check that your e-mail system supports off-line working.

EXERCISE 37

**Sending an
e-mail message**

■ Duration: 1 hour

1   Click on **Compose** and **New Message** and the message pad
    (Figure 82) will appear. Explore the other message option (**New
    Message using**), which is available within the **Compose** menu.
    This provides some attractive standard messages.

2   If you do not know anyone with e-mail to whom you can send a
    message, you can always send yourself an e-mail. This allows
    you to see what it looks like when it arrives. The other choice is
    to send a message to a public body. BBC Television and Radio
    have a number of programmes which encourage viewers and
    listeners to send them e-mails. Why not combine your practice
    with sending the programme your views?

3   Complete the message pad with either an original message or
    the message below:

    To:
    cc:
    BCC:
    Subject: Trying out e-mail

    **This message is my first e-mail. I am experimenting with how
    to send messages.**

    Best wishes,

4   When you have completed your message, send it by clicking on
    the **Send** icon.

5   Practise sending messages until you are confident.

How to read your mail

It is easy to check your mail. With Outlook Express you
access the Internet and click on the **Send/Receive** button. This
will retrieve all your mail. Don't worry about where it is
stored at the moment. There are many things about e-mail
which you do not need to know yet. Just accept that it works.

    If you want to, you can check your mail automatically by
setting the system. You do this by choosing the **Tools** menu
and selecting the **Options** item. This allows you to set the
system to check your mail automatically at regular intervals

and even make a sound to tell you when mail has been delivered. This seems a great idea until you have spent a day with the computer pinging every few minutes – then you never use it again!

Your mail is presented to you as a list of subject titles and names of people who have sent you a message. You choose the ones you want to read by clicking on them. The names are usually e-mail names, which may be different from actual names. Here is a typical list of received e-mails. This list is normally called the Inbox.

From	Subject
Ji	Visit to Leeds
Lionheart	Make lots of money
Jcollins	Can you help
MusicShop	Your order is ready
Bikenewsgroup	New parts for old

How do you reply to e-mail?

Once you have clicked on the mail you want to read, you can do several things with it. The options available are:

1   Read and delete the message:
     File menu, select **Delete**.

2   Read and save the message to a folder:
     File menu, select **Copy to a Folder**.
     This leaves the original message in your Inbox.

3   Read and move the message to a folder:
     File menu, select **Move to a Folder**.
     This removes the message from your Inbox.

4   Read and reply:
     Compose menu/button, select **Reply to Author**.
     When you reply to a message the original text is usually retained; if you then get a response to your reply, the original message and your reply are both retained. Figure 83 shows how e-mails can grow. It can be useful to see the whole conversation but when the messages are long they can be confusing. In addition, different people write their replies in different places – some reply at the end of messages while others respond at the beginning.

```
Hi Alan

Thanks for your reply - I will see you at the corner of
the High Street and Bank Avenue.

Cheers

John

Dear John

I would like to have a drink with you. What about meeting
on 15th March? Could you suggest a place to meet? It would
need to be about 7pm.

Best Wishes,

Alan

Hi Alan

Long time since we had a night out. What about going for
a drink? Could you suggest a date and time?

Cheers

John
```

FIGURE 83 *E-mail messages can grow very rapidly!*

The subject remains the same when you reply except that the word 'Re' is placed in front of the title (e.g. Re-Example), indicating it is a reply. If you reply to the reply then another 'Re' is added (e.g. Re-Re-Example).

5 Read and reply to everyone:
Compose menu/button, select **Reply to All**.
This is similar to Replying to Author but your reply is sent to everyone to whom the original message was sent. A copy of the original message is left in the Inbox.

6 Read and forward:
Compose menu/button, select **Forward**.
This allows you to pass your message to a third party. A copy of the original message is left in the Inbox.

These functions are available in most e-mail systems. The examples here all relate to Outlook Express. If you are using another product, explore the Menu items and you will find these options.

EXERCISE 38

Receiving and replying to an e-mail

■ Duration: 30 minutes

1 You may already be receiving e-mail messages, but if you have not been sent any the first step is to send yourself a message. Even if you have no other messages, many ISPs send new customers messages about how to use their e-mail service. You can use these to carry out the exercises listed here.

2 Open Microsoft Outlook (Figure 81), select the inbox and double-click on a message in your inbox. You should see a list of items from which you can choose. Some e-mail systems show the messages in bold when they have not been read and remove the bold once they have. Your selected message will open and you can read the e-mail.

3 Click on **Compose** when you are ready to reply. This menu provides you with four ways to do this – **Reply to Author**, **Reply to All**, **Forward** and **Forward as Attachment**. Use all the options except Forward as an Attachment, which will be explained later.

4 If you are sending e-mails make sure the person receiving the e-mail is happy for you to practise using them, otherwise send genuine e-mails. If you are taking part in a course your fellow students should be willing to help.

5 Experiment with the position of your reply (i.e. before or after the original message).

6 Continue until you feel you understand the process of reading and replying to e-mails.

How do you attach files to messages?

A very important feature of all e-mail systems is the ability to attach files. This allows you to insert word processing, spreadsheet, database and graphic files into your messages. However, this does assume that the person you are sending your message to has a copy of the application so that he can read the file. It is a common event to get a reply saying that the recipient cannot read your attachment and could you send it in another format? One simple way, if it is a word processing file, is to copy and paste it into the main body of your e-mail. Microsoft Outlook is a Windows application so it is easy to copy and paste items into the message pad from applications such as Word.

Another problem is that e-mail attachments can be damaged (**corrupted**) by being sent over the Internet so that they cannot be read. This is caused by a number of factors but again leads to replies asking you to send it again. It might not be possible to send attachments to some addresses.

If you are receiving e-mails with attachments you need to be aware of the problem of computer viruses. Some files (especially those with the extensions .exe, .doc, .dot and .xls) attached to messages may carry viruses. You need to judge who has sent you the file (do you know and trust them?) and whether the virus protection you have on your system is adequate.

Attaching a file using Outlook is straightforward. On the toolbar is an icon which resembles a paper clip. If you click on this icon a window will open which allows you to select any file. This is inserted below your message. Figure 84 shows an e-mail message with an attached file.

| Tutorial 21 | → | The address book |

How do you use the address book?

The e-mail address book (an example is shown in Figure 85) serves the same purpose as its paper equivalent. It is a place to store information about your friends, colleagues and contacts. However, it has a number of extra features which will help you send e-mails. You access the address book by clicking on the **Address Book** button (Figure 81) on the button bar.

The address book allows you to store multiple e-mail addresses for an individual (many people often have several e-mail accounts – currently I have three). It provides you with the facilities to send e-mail directly to any address you have indicated (highlighted) by clicking on **Tools** and then **Send Mail**. The message pad will appear (Figure 82) with the

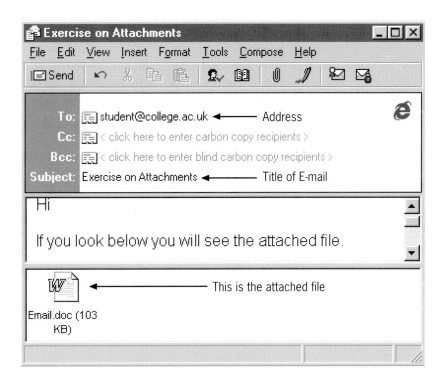

FIGURE 84 *Attaching files to e-mail*

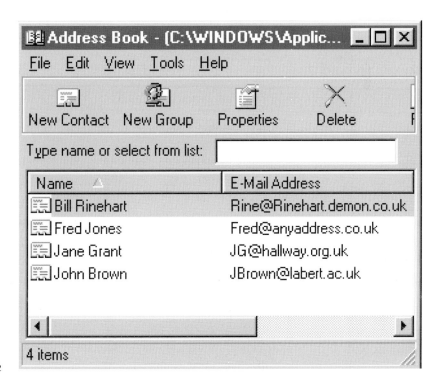

FIGURE 85 *Address book*

address line completed. You just type in the message you want to send.

You can store home and work addresses, telephone and fax numbers in the address book. In addition, it is possible to include Internet addresses and links to the sites directly from the address book.

The address book also offers you the ability to create groups. There are a number of contacts to whom you can simultaneously send e-mail messages by sending just one to the group. This is a very useful function as it can save you a lot of time sending duplicate messages. A group can be established by clicking on the **New Group** button and either selecting from the existing addresses in the book or entering new addresses to include in the group. Groups need to be given a name so that by sending an e-mail to this (group) name you send messages to all its members. Figure 86 shows you the New Group creation screen.

Other main functions of the address book are:

■ importing addresses – they can be taken with you from other applications which export the same type of text file (e.g. Microsoft Exchange)

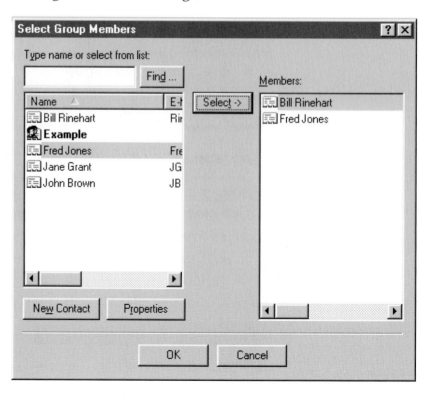

FIGURE 86 *New group creation in Outlook*

■ creating electronic business cards

■ printing – you can print all or selected parts of your address book.

EXERCISE 39

Adding addresses

■ Duration: 30 minutes

1 Click on **Address Book** and then **New Contact**. A window called Properties appears, which is essentially a blank page of the address book (Figure 87).

2 Explore the different pages by clicking on the tabs (e.g. **Home**) to see what information the address book can contain. When you are confident that you have gained a good awareness of the contents return to the **Personal** page (click on the **Personal** tab) and enter the following new contacts.

John William Brown (Nickname – Birdie)
jwb@anyplace.co.uk

Ann Jenkins (Nickname – Allie)
AnnJ@blank.org.uk

Arthur Jamsa (No nickname)
Jamsa@college.ac.uk

3 Observe what happens when you enter the e-mail addresses. You should see changes to the **Add** button. When you have finished an entry click on **OK** to see what happens, then repeat

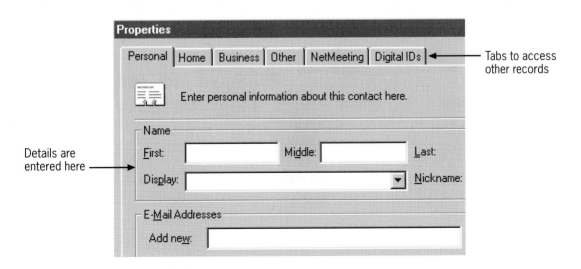

FIGURE 87 *Address book properties*

the operation. Try the options (e.g. click on **Add**) and observe what happens.

Finding an e-mail address

If you are seeking a telephone number, you can pick up a directory or ring Directory Enquiries. Looking up an e-mail address is different. There is no one place which will give you all e-mail addresses. However, there are many ways to find the address you want. All the major search engines offer the option of searching for an individual or organisation e-mail address. In addition, there are specialist directories, usually called White and Yellow Pages, which list addresses. In simple terms, White Pages list individual e-mail addresses and web sites, Yellow Pages list organisation addresses and sites.

Most of the directories offer both White and Yellow Pages. Two well known directories are:

- Bigfoot (Figure 88)
- Four11 (Figure 89).

Searching for an e-mail address is very similar to using an Internet search engine. In practice, you can use a search engine to locate an e-mail address and many web sites inform you of the e-mail address, so it is worth visiting the web site of an organisation.

FIGURE 88 *Bigfoot directory*

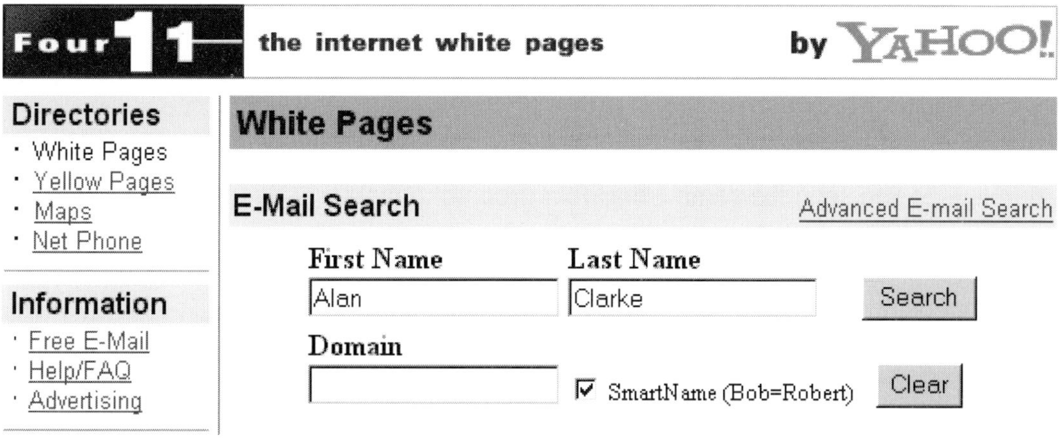

FIGURE 89 *Four11 directory*

What next?

E-mail is a powerful means of communication. Now that you have an insight into how to use it why not join some mail or news group and start to use e-mail every day? Unfortunately, there are some drawbacks to e-mail such as receiving advertisements rather like the postal junk mail. In some cases these can be offensive. Most responsible advertisers, however, will tell you how to remove yourself from their lists.

SELF TEST QUESTIONS

If you want to test your understanding of this chapter try to answer these questions. The answers are given at the end of the book.

1 What is e-mail?

2 How much does e-mail cost?

3 What do you need to be able to send e-mail?

4 Give the general structure of an e-mail address.

5 List three of the key functions of an e-mail system.

SELF TEST QUESTIONS – continued

6 What are angry e-mails called?

7 What can you attach or insert into an e-mail message?

8 How do you send the same e-mail to a group of people?

9 What sort of information can you store in an e-mail address book?

10 What is the general name of the e-mail directories?

Answers

Chapter 1: Foundation

1 Desktop and tower, laptop and palmtop.
2 Floppy disk drive.
3 One character (e.g. a letter or a number).
4 This is the name given to the standard English keyboard. It is called this because part of the top line of keys spells QWERTY.
5 Maximise.
6 It loads automatically when you switch the computer on.
7 By clicking on the appropriate icon or on Start and Programs and then selecting the application from the list displayed by clicking on it.
8 A letter in the name is underlined (e.g. File).
9 On floppy disk or CD-ROM.
10 An extension comprising a full stop and three letters (e.g. .exe).

Chapter 2: Word processing

1 An I bar.
2 The text automatically moves on to another line. This is called word wrap.
3 Press enter or return.
4 You would go into Page Setup and alter what you want.
5 Extra space left in a document's margins so that the pages can be bound together.
6 The passage is aligned so that all the words finish at the right-hand margin, and the text at the left is uneven.
7 Undo.
8 Insert and overwrite.
9 Clip art.
10 Search for and change characters, words or phrases in a document.

Chapter 3: Spreadsheets

1 Row, column and cell.
2 It becomes a plus sign (+).
3 The fill handle.
4 *
5 C8/M11.
6 By using the toolbar icons; see Figure 41.
7 Use the Autoformat function (Figure 42).
8 There are toolbar icons to help you do this.
9 Highlight the area.
10 Anywhere – for example, business, home, school.

Chapter 4: Databases

1 Tables.
2 Fields.
3 A Wizard is a device which allows you to create databases or other objects more easily by choosing between options.
4 A spreadsheet.
5 A database in which related information is stored in one place (i.e. a table).
6 A field is an individual item of data (e.g. surname).
7 A record is a group of fields which make up an entire piece of information (e.g. name and address).
8 Tables are often related by having one field that relates to all the fields in a second table.
9 Text, numbers, date/time, currency, autonumber, yes/no, and OLE objects.
10 Find, sort, queries and reports.

Chapter 5: Painting and drawing

1 A set of images which you can buy. Many are given away free with magazines.
2 You can copy and paste images from Paint into other Windows applications.
3 There are many. Choose any three from: pencil, line, curved line, rectangle, ellipse, rounded rectangle, polygon, eraser, palette, paint brush, paint dropper, selection tools and magnifier.
4 Pixels.
5 You can draw up to five different thicknesses of lines.
6 Clipboard Viewer.
7 In the palette.
8 Irregular and rectangular.
9 By using the colour editor. It allows you to mix new shades and include them in the palette.
10 Bitmap – .bmp.

Chapter 6: The Internet

1 Electronic mail (e-mail), telnet, file transfer protocol (FTP), mailgroups, newsgroups (often called Usenet), chat and the World Wide Web (WWW).
2 Microsoft Internet Explorer and Netscape Navigator.
3 Universal resource locator.
4 Hypertext markup language, or HTML.
5 Internet service provider.
6 Hyperlinks.
7 It becomes a hand.
8 A web site you have included in your favourites list so that you can access it easily by clicking on the entry.
9 HotBot is a search engine. It helps you to find web pages which meet your needs.
10 A group of e-mail users. You send an e-mail to a standard address, and it will be sent to everyone in the group.

Chapter 7: E-mail

1 E-mail is a world-wide electronic postal service. It is a major part of the Internet.

2 Very little – the cost of a telephone call to access the message (usually a local call) and a proportion of the costs of having access to the Internet.

3 An address, an electronic post box and postal service which is provided by the ISP.

4 name@organisation.type.country
   Name   Organisation   Type   Country

5 Inbox (letter box), Outbox (mail tray in an office), Compose (write your message), Send (post your letter into postbox), Receive (pick up your mail) and Address book.

6 Flaming or flames.

7 Files.

8 Group under a common name in your address book all the people to whom you want to send that e-mail.

9 The e-mail address, name, home and business addresses, telephone numbers, fax numbers and nicknames.

10 White and Yellow Pages.

Glossary

Application A software program designed to perform a task such as word processing, sending e-mail or preparing spreadsheets.

Boot This is the process that occurs when you switch on the computer. It involves automatic loading of the operating system (e.g. Windows 95) and checking of the equipment to ensure that everything is ready for you to use.

Browser A browser is an application which allows you to access a World Wide Web site. Each site has a unique address which is called a uniform resource locator (URL), which, when entered into the browser, allows it to find the site and view its contents.

Byte The basic measure of memory. A byte is sufficient memory to store one character (e.g. a letter or a number).

CD-ROM Stands for compact disc read-only memory: the computer equivalent of an audio compact disc and used to store large amounts of information.

CD-RW This is a specialist form of CD-ROM which allows information to be both read from the disc and written to it.

Clipboard A special area of memory in which applications in Windows 95 can store information. Material cut and copied from a document is stored on the clipboard in order to paste from it later.

Clip art Standard images that you can buy, or which are given away free with computer magazines. Thousands of clip art images can be loaded into applications such as Microsoft Word or Paint.

CPU The central processing unit is a silicon chip which controls the operation of the computer.

Desktop This is the main display of the operating system and is normally the first display you see after the computer has loaded the operating system (e.g. Windows).

Desktop computer A computer that consists of a monitor, keyboard, mouse and a large box which contains the computer's engine – the CPU, magnetic (hard) disk and drives.

Dialog box A window that appears on your screen to allow the computer system to communicate with you. Often dialog boxes offer you choices, warn you of problems or report errors.

Directory A list of World Wide Web addresses related to a particular topic or subject.

Downloading   Transferring a file from a web site or remote computer to your own computer.

Extension (or file extension)   Tells you what type of software a file holds (examples include .doc, .txt, .rtf, which are all text files).

Field   An individual piece of information stored on a database, usually as part of a record.

File   A collection of digital (computer) information. There are many types of file – word processing, graphic, spreadsheet etc.

Flame   An angry e-mail message.

Floppy disk   A small magnetic disk on which you can store a small amount of information in the form of files.

Folder   A location on the computer in which you can store files.

Footer   Essentially a standard item which is placed on the bottom of each page when word processing. It is often a graphic image such as a company logo but it can be text only or a mixture of text and graphics (*see also* Header).

Font   Characters can be printed and displayed in many different styles. These styles are known as fonts.

Format   A way of structuring the computer information stored in a file on a disk or drive. There are many different types of file format.

FTP   Stands for file transfer protocol. It is the means by which you can transfer a file of information from one web site to another or to your own computer.

Gb   Gigabyte – a measure of memory (approximately one billion bytes of information).

Greyed out   An icon or menu item that is faded, meaning that the option is not currently available.

GUI   Stands for graphical user interface. Windows 95 is a GUI-type display in which icons, windows and a mouse pointer interact to produce an easy to use environment.

Gutter   The extra space allowed in the margin for pages to be bound together.

Hard disk   Magnetic disk which is located inside the computer on which a large amount of information can be stored.

Hardware   The physical components of a computer.

Header   Essentially a standard item which is placed on the top of each page (*see* Footer).

Highlighting   A way of selecting material on screen by clicking, holding down and moving the mouse button. The highlighted item normally changes colour to show it has been chosen.

HTML   Hypertext markup language is a specialist language which is used to design documents and sites on the World Wide Web so that they can be read using a browser.

Hypertext   Pages of a web site are linked together through a number of hypertext connections. These are shown by underlined words, coloured words, icons and graphic pictures. The links allow the user to jump between different parts of the site or even between sites.

Icon   A small picture which represents a computer function or operation.

IRC   The original home of chat is Internet Relay Chat, which is a separate part of the Internet with its own computers and systems.

ISP   Internet service providers are commercial companies who provide connections to the Internet for individuals and companies.

Justification   A way of laying out text – left, right, centred or fully justified. For example, left justification means that text is aligned so that its left edge is parallel with the paper's edge.

Kb   A Kilobyte is a measure of memory (1024 bytes).

Laptop   A portable computer with a screen built into its cover.

LCD   Stands for liquid crystal display. A type of screen used in some portable computers.

Maximise   To expand a window so that it fills all of the screen. A window is maximised by clicking on the small button with a rectangle inside, situated at the top right-hand corner of the window.

Mb   A Megabyte is a measure of computer memory (approximately one million bytes).

Memory   A measure of a computer's capacity to perform tasks and to store information.

Menu   A method of displaying options.

Minimise   To shrink a window down to a button in order to make space on the screen. A window is minimised by clicking on the small button with a horizontal line inside it, situated at the top right-hand corner of the window.

MHz   The symbol for megahertz: this is a measure of the speed of the computer.

Motherboard   The main circuit board within the computer.

Mouse   An input device that is used to control an on-screen pointer. The pointer is moved left, right, up or down by moving the mouse in the chosen direction. To select an item on the monitor the mouse has one, two or three buttons that you press (click) to make your choice.

Multitasking   Carrying out several tasks in parallel. Windows 95 allows you to undertake multitasking.

Operating system   Software provides the instructions to make the hardware work and allows specific tasks such as communicating with the Internet or word processing to be performed. Computers need to match hardware and software together, and to ensure that the match is exact a special software program is needed. This is the operating system.

Palmtop   A small battery-powered pocket-sized computer which usually does not have all the functions of either a laptop or a desktop computer.

PC   Stands for personal computer.

Pixel   Graphic images are made up of many small rectangular dots called pixels.

PoP   Internet service providers provide you with a telephone number which is called a point of presence (PoP). Your communication software dials this number when you try to access the Internet and links you through your modem to the ISP's computer. The ISP is linked to the Internet. Many ISPs have several PoPs throughout the country.

QWERTY   The name given to a standard English keyboard. The first few letters of the top line of alphabetical keys on the keyboard are QWERTY.

Radio button   Standard Windows 95 features. They appear as small circles alongside lists of items. You select the option you want by clicking in the appropriate circle; this places a dot inside the circle, to tell you the option has been chosen. When you close down your Windows system you need to select from three options with radio buttons (Shut Down, Restart or Restart in MSDOS).

RAM   Random Access Memory: the computer's working memory in which the computer carries out its functions once it is switched on. It exists only while the machine is on. If the power is switched off, so is the memory.

Record   A group of related fields of information which you normally find in a database.

Relational database   A database in which related information is stored in one place. In Microsoft Access all related information is stored in the same table. Most modern databases are relational.

ROM   Read-only memory – the computer's permanent memory and built into the structure of the silicon chips inside it. It is not lost if the power is switched off.

Scrolling   In Windows 95 you will often find that the display is bigger than the screen and you cannot see it all at once. In order to see the whole contents you have to move around the display. To do this use the display bars at the right-hand side and along the bottom of the display. Clicking on the up, down, left or right-pointing arrows will move you in that direction. This is called scrolling, and the bars are called scroll bars.

Search engine   An application that allows you to search for a web page containing information on a specific topic.

Software   Computer programs written to allow you or the computer to carry out certain tasks, such as constructing databases.

Spam   Unsolicited e-mails, often advertisements.

Surfing   The process of wandering around the World Wide Web in search of interesting information.

Table   Part of a database on which information is stored as a series of records and fields.

Toolbar   Often appears at the top of an application (e.g. Word) display and contains many icons and buttons which connect you to the different functions of that application.

Uploading   Transferring a file from your computer to a web site or remote computer.

URL   The URL (uniform resource locator) is the unique address of a World Wide Web site that allows a browser to locate the site.

VDU   Visual display unit – another term for monitor.

Virus   A computer program designed to cause harm to a computer.

Web site   A collection of pages on the Internet.

World Wide Web (WWW)   A collection of millions of web sites and documents spread across the world as part of the Internet.

Window   A rectangular area of the screen in which computer applications and information is displayed.

Wizard   Many Windows 95/98 applications include a Wizard. Wizards are used to perform complex tasks more easily by allowing the user to choose between options.

Word wrap (wrapping)   When you enter text into a word processor or other application it will automatically start a new line when it needs to, without you doing anything.

Index